Basic Floristry

A First Textbook for Student Flower Designers

RONA COLEMAN S.F. Dip. A.I.F.D.

Illustrations by Ken and Doreen Spring

DAVID & CHARLES

NEWTON ABBOT LONDON VANCOUVER

o 7153 6561 4

First published in Great Britain by
Pelham Books Ltd

Revised edition published by
David & Charles (Holdings) Limited 1974

Printed in Great Britain
for David & Charles (Holdings) Limited
South Devon House Newton Abbot Devon

Published in Canada by Douglas David & Charles Limited
3645 McKechnie Drive West Vancouver BC

CONTENTS

LIST OF PLATES

Foreword

This textbook is intended to supplement practical work-room experience and formal instruction in Schools of Floristry, day-release classes and so on.

It is intended, too, as a guide to parents, as the ultimate success of the student is largely dependent on the support and encouragement of the family.

It is also hoped that it will shed light on the Flower Industry as a progressive career for both boys and girls as they leave school or technical college.

In its early stages, a career in the world of flowers is not always as immediately financially rewarding as many other careers at the same stage, but the scope of opportunity is manifold.

Since preparing this book in its first edition eight years ago, there has been a remarkable change in some aspects of our world of flowers. Most recently, we have entered the Common Market and all our measurements, therefore, are decimalised. In this new edition of *Basic Floristry*, the familiar wire gauge sizes are replaced by their metric equivalent. There is a complete conversion table given on page 8.

Flower counts in most wholesale markets have also changed and wherever possible, this information has been brought up to date. The challenge of better growing, wider distribution and highly competitive selling techniques is not merely a succession of words on a page. It is a reality, reflecting the mood of the action-packed times in which we live.

The student who qualifies can look forward to a career which can be followed at any age, in any country and which, by its particular nature, remains ever-changing, absorbing and challenging.

Flower Design   RONA COLEMAN
of Britain

UNIT OF WEIGHT
Price £x per 25 kg.

SIZES		LENGTHS	
Recommended	Replacing	Recommended	Replacing
1.25mm.	18s.w.g.	90mm.	$3\frac{1}{2}$in.
1.00mm.	19s.w.g.	100mm.	4in.
0.90mm.	20s.w.g.	130mm.	5in.
0.71mm.	22s.w.g.	150mm.	6in.
0.56mm.	24s.w.g.	180mm.	7in.
0.46mm.	26s.w.g.	200mm.	8in.
0.38mm.	28s.w.g.	230mm.	9in.
0.32mm.	30s.w.g	260mm.	10in.
0.28mm.	32s.w.g.	310mm.	12in.
0.24mm.	34s.w.g.	360mm.	14in.
0.20mm.	36s.w.g.	380mm.	15in.
		460mm.	18in.

BUNDLES
Weight per bundle $= 2\frac{1}{2}$ kg.

REELS
125 grams per reel.
10 reels per box.
20 boxes per 25 kg. pack.

CHAPTER ONE

Introduction to Commercial Flower Design

What exactly is Flower Design? It involves the preparation and presentation of cut flowers, foliage and plants ready for sale. It usually implies sale to the general public, but many florists also have contract decorating work for firms, hotels, shops and offices.

To do all this efficiently, the Flower Designer must have a thorough understanding of every aspect of the work, and be able to execute designs as quickly as possible. As they arrive from the grower, cut flowers have to be conditioned for use, cared for in storage and presented for sale in whatever form the customer wishes.

This involves, needless to say, a good knowledge of what flowers are available at all seasons of the year, which ones are most suitable for any particular work and, of course, the technical ability to make the finished presentation look attractive and acceptable to the customer.

During your first week in a florist's workroom, you will no doubt see a number of new and strange materials which you will want to understand as quickly as possible.

Every industry has raw materials which have to be processed or treated before they can be offered for sale. The flower industry is no exception. The cut flowers arrive in your shop, possibly from a local nursery, perhaps by air freight from the other side of the world, but they all have to be unpacked and cared for expertly by the florist before they are ready for use or direct sale.

During your first week or so, you will probably not be allowed to handle any of the flowers. This is not unusual, so do not be disheartened and immediately imagine that you will never get to the stage of being allowed to design a bridal bouquet. If, by any chance, you have already done some preliminary training in a nursery, you will already be accustomed to handling living material. If not, it takes a little time to acquire the necessary touch, and the senior florist will quite rightly want you to begin right at the beginning, learning all you can, slowly but surely.

You will find it a great help if you have a small pocket notebook so that in any spare moment you can make notes on everything you see. For instance, the names and varieties of flowers and foliage in general use, the various phrases used to explain the work, any designs you see being made, with a rough sketch whenever possible. It is amazing how quickly these notes will increase and how helpful they are in assisting your memory. At the end of twelve months you will have been through every growing season, and you should then have a pretty good idea of what is available month by month in your particular area.

During your initial interview with your employer, he or she will probably have told you what type of overall you should wear. Some firms like to keep to a standard design which you either buy yourself or which is supplied to you. Other firms do not mind as long as the overall is always neat and clean. There is such a wide choice of colour and weight now that even if you can afford only one, those made in man-made fibres wash and drip-dry easily overnight. At least one pocket is essential and make sure you always have a pencil or ball-point pen handy. Use the type that flicks in or out with a spring – they can be bought at any stationer's for as little as five pence – and take care that you always have the point retracted when it is in your pocket. The ink is indelible and will soon spoil the appearance of a new overall.

At the beginning of your training you may never actually be visible to the public, but take your usual pride in your appearance, nevertheless. Being a student flower designer does not mean that you will be spending all your time knee-deep in damp moss, and the day must come when quite suddenly you are called into the shop to wait on a customer, or perhaps to go out and help with an important decoration. So arrive for work each day ready for the unexpected and one day it will happen.

Working with flowers and wire is undoubtedly rather hard on the hands, but they only need just a little extra care. Some people wear a barrier cream to prevent hands from getting stained and others wear rubber gloves when mossing frames. At any rate, you will find that you need to use more hand cream than before and the extra money spent on a good preparation will prove a good investment. If you like lacquered nails, use a fairly pale colour and make sure you always keep it looking impeccably neat.

Most flower shops have to be kept considerably cooler than the average room or office, for obvious reasons. On warm days they frequently seem quite cold by comparison with the outside atmosphere, so dress a little more warmly than you would normally. When choosing your overall remember to leave plenty of room for an extra jacket or pullover underneath. Unless you are desperate, never put it OVER the overall, the general effect is most unprofessional.

The majority of florists need to work standing up for most of the day, so make sure you are wearing very comfortable shoes. For the coldest months you can buy lambswool interlining socks for about fifty pence, and these will keep your feet really warm.

As you can imagine, the day-to-day work in a flower shop involves quite a lot of exercise, and it is very likely that you will be more hungry than usual! Take an extra snack to eat at lunch and tea break otherwise you will find yourself drooping long before closing time.

No employer will expect a student florist to understand the routine and all about the flowers and equipment at once. Make sure, however, that you do understand what you are asked to do before you begin. If you do not fully comprehend – ASK. Never be afraid to ask questions.

It is far more aggravating if a student pretends to understand and goes ahead and completes a particular operation all wrong. This results in loss of valuable time and equipment. You are certain to make mistakes, but remember that somewhere, sometime, each senior designer has also had to learn from the beginning.

Master each stage as thoroughly as possible. Keep a smile ready and do what you are asked cheerfully and as well as you know how. This way lies success – and in the world of flowers there is plenty of room at the top.

CHAPTER TWO

Wires and General Equipment

The florist uses wire to support the flower stems and also to give the design more stability than it would have if all the stems were left to go their own way.

Needless to say, this does not mean that heavy wires must be used so that the flowers become so rigid that they lose all their natural appeal. It is most important that a flower design never looks 'manufactured'. Nevertheless, since bouquets, funeral tributes and so forth have to put· up with a certain amount of handling, the good florist will be able to choose the correct gauge of wire so as to give the design the right amount of support – no more and no less.

Only experience and practice will help you to know instinctively which wire is needed, but the first step towards this ideal is a thorough knowledge of the wires that are in general use. There are, in fact, three types of wire in use in the workroom.

1. The *wire frames*, which form the bases of most funeral designs.
2. *The stub wires*, which are used for supporting and mounting flowers and foliage. These are bought by weight, cut to length. Thus, a bundle of thick wires will contain fewer than a bundle of finer ones of similar length. They are very expensive and that is one good reason for always trying to use the right

length and gauge. It is inevitable that a small amount may have to be cut off after some. flowers have been wired, but if this is more than an inch or so, quite a bit of profit will have been swept into the rubbish bin by the end of a week's work!

3. *Reel wire* is available in both heavy and fine gauges. It is bought on wooden spools which, when empty, make excellent fire lighters. The heavier reel wire is used for binding moss on to the wire frames; the lighter gauges are for wiring small flowers, such as Lily-of-the-Valley.

Gauges. Wires are sized in a similar way to knitting needles. That is to say, the higher the number, the finer is the wire. The thickest wire in general use is 1.25mm whilst the finest is gauge 0.20mm. Between these two extremes, there are the sizes in most general use in day-to-day floristry. The use of particular gauges will vary somewhat from district to district, and most shops stock the range that is found to be most useful for the area and the work in demand.

The wires in most general use are between 1.00, 0.90 and 0.71mm. The 1.25mm. size is used for heavy-headed flowers like Chrysanthemums. The other sizes are for medium-weight flowers. 0.56 to 0.45mm. gauges are used for delicate flowers such as Freesia, Hyacinth and Stephanotis, and for wiring separate leaves for corsages and bouquets.

Wire storage. Most florists store their wires in heavy-based containers which must be tall enough to support the bundle properly without being easily knocked over. Picking up wires which have been accidentally scattered all over the floor is a most tedious job, and it stands to reason that a set-back of this kind will not create a very happy atmosphere in a busy workroom. It will help if each container is clearly labelled with the number of the gauge contained therein. It is permissible to mix different *lengths* of wire which are the same gauge, but never mix *different gauges* in the same container. When designers are working quickly, they will want to find the necessary wires as speedily as possible, and a lot of time can be lost if the gauges are mixed up.

Incidentally, both reel and stub wire should be kept dry. If allowed to become damp it rusts easily and then makes both hands and flower material dirty. It is also possible to buy green plastic-covered wire, and some florists use this almost exclusively, but it is more expensive.

String is a basic part of workroom equipment. It is used for binding funeral sheaves, or for binding moss on to the funeral frames. Some designers use ordinary brown string, whilst others prefer the green dyed twine, of which there are several varieties and thicknesses.

Floratape and Guttapercha. This is also an expensive item of equipment which must not be wasted. It is a finishing tape which is available in various colours. It is used mainly for bouquets and corsages and seals the end of the stem or the base of the flower, thus helping the design to stay fresher for longer. It also makes a very neat finish to the design. The various greens are the colours in most general use, because they give the most natural finish. However, some designers like to use pink, white, lemon or blue or other delicate tints to match the flowers they are using.

Foam base. This is a material used in the preparation

15

of vase designs. It must be thoroughly soaked in clean water before being used. It should not, however, be kept in water, otherwise when heavy stems are put into it, it may break apart. If you are asked to put a few blocks to soak, remember to take them out before you go home at night.

Scissors and knives. Probably your firm will supply you with scissors. Make sure you look after them carefully. They are expensive and it is very easy to lose them in a sack of rubbish or pile of foliage. Mark your own pair with either a name tape, or by fixing a piece of tape round one of the handles. Never borrow other people's scissors. It is most provoking to put out your hand for your scissors and find that someone has laid them down on the other side of the workroom.

You will probably be expected to provide your own knife. This can cost you at least one pound for a good one, so do not lay it down thoughtlessly. Things get swept away so quickly with the rubbish.

Keep a small duster or hand towel either in your pocket or near at hand. It is impossible to keep either your hands or the workbench dry all the time and it can save lots of steps to and fro if you have one with you.

Other general equipment in a flower shop includes *cards*, *ribbons*, *wrapping paper*, *corsage boxes*, *pins*, etc. It may possibly be the job of the student florist to see that supplies of these are always available. Whatever small task is given to you, see that you do it properly. It may seem insignificant to you at first, but imagine, a well-made corsage is no use to the client unless it is equipped with at least one pin, an expensive funeral tribute is meaningless without a

Plate 1 (*above*) Some examples of flower design equipment. Notice especially the sharp well-balanced shears which together with the knife are your most important pieces of equipment; *Plate 2* (*below*) Rona Coleman explains that a design should always have movement and must never look stiff or artificial. Notice the bowl of clean water to keep the wired and taped foliage fresh.

Plate 3 (left) Carnations and large chrysanthemums are difficult to use on account of their size. As a general rule allow each flower plenty of space and be careful to check each stem length before cutting; *Plate 4 (right)* Arum lilies look just as well in a home arrangement as in a church pedestal. Their own foliage makes an excellent design. Do make sure they have plenty of water. Here they are supported with wire mesh in an Italian pottery pitcher.

card. If these accessories are not readily to hand, time, patience and perhaps a good client can be lost, and it could be your fault!

Ribbons, perhaps, come into a special category of their own. They form one of the most glamorous parts of the florist's equipment and they are also one of the most expensive. But whatever the quantity or variety of ribbon kept in stock, it must always be in good order. If you are asked to cut a length of ribbon, cut it neatly, so that the next person does not have to waste a piece by having to trim the end first. Some florists use pinking shears, which make a very neat cut. When you put the reel back into stock, fix the loose end with a small piece of sellotape to prevent the ribbon from unwinding.

Wrapping paper, particularly if it is printed, is a very costly item. Broadly speaking, it costs at least five pence to wrap an average-sized parcel of flowers. Add to this the cost of the message card and envelope, as well as the necessary care cards, and you will soon understand the reason for economy.

Each shop has its particular method of wrapping and you will in time be shown how this should be done. Although you should wrap with economy, it is worse still to be too mean, because a client who gets water from the stems in his shoes as he walks along the street is not likely to come back in a hurry. You must try to strike the happy medium between using too small a piece of paper and using much more than necessary. It is very depressing for the person who has to pay the bills – your employer – to see paper carelessly torn off the roll, ribbon badly trimmed or any other of the aggravating little extravagances that can add up so frighteningly throughout a year.

Once in a while it does no harm to pretend that it's *your* shop. This means, of course, that the invoices will belong to *you*. If you can stretch your imagination this far, it won't be difficult for you to sympathise with your employer's point of view.

CHAPTER THREE

Mossing and Preparation
of Frames

Mossing frames for funeral designs is a task which almost always falls on the junior florists, but it is not by any means an unimportant one. The correct preparation of a frame makes all the difference, not only to the speed with which the design can be made, but to the finished work. Some florists prefer to buy their frames ready-mossed, but many others always prepare their own, for quite a number of reasons. Most shops keep a fairly good selection of frames in stock, and these can be stored almost indefinitely. Once mossed, however, they not only take up much more space, but they do not keep very well for much longer than a week.

The quality of the moss will vary quite a bit in relation to the locality of the shop. Where moss has to be despatched to the large wholesale markets it is usually packed either into sacks or polythene bags. It should never be used dry, and although the top layer is usually fairly damp, the underneath may be almost bone dry. Wires will never drive easily into a frame that has been prepared with dry moss.

The florist has usually developed his own way of ensuring that the moss is damp enough. For instance, if he has nursery or garden space, the whole sack can be soaked in a tank and then left to drain in the open air. If the shop has no garden premises, then the moss must be soaked in small quantities, probably in the workroom. One thing to remember for your own comfort – if the moss sacks are stored outside, always have at least one indoors during the winter months. Moss holds frost for a long time and it is a very miserable job trying to prepare a frame with frozen moss!

Method. The moss is packed in the bag in small bundles. These must be teased out and loosened, and all stones, sticks, etc., removed. Using either wire or string – whichever is the general practice in your shop – attach the binding material to the wire frame. The raised side of the frame should be uppermost. Take a handful of moss in your left hand, place it on the frame and secure with one turn of the wire. If you are right-handed, work from right to left, feeding in the moss with the left hand and binding with the right, turning the frame as you go. After each turn of the binding wire, give it a smart tug to make sure the base will be firm. The wire should be about half an inch apart, evenly spaced all round the frame. If you do not bind as closely as this, the moss may shift and the base will not be firm enough (Fig. 1).

You may find, at first, that the moss tends to get pushed inwards towards the inner ring of the frame. Make a point of ensuring that this does not happen, because the outer edge must have its fair share of moss to form adequate support for the flowers and foliage. It is largely a matter of personal preference how thickly the moss must be put on the frame, but the florist who is helping you will give you an idea of what is wanted.

As a general rule, heavy flowers such as Gladioli and

Preparation of Frames

Chrysanthemums will need a slightly denser moss base than lighter flowers like Daffodils, Iris or Carnations.

You will probably begin by mossing a small ring or wreath frame. The moss must be put on evenly all the way round – no bumps or thin places. This will be much easier if you get into a rhythm of working. If you stop for any reason, you may find a thin place or gap where you have taken up your work again.

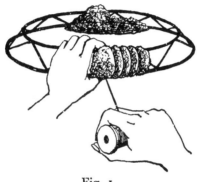

Fig. 1.

Memorial Cross. The two most usual designs for formal tributes are the round wreath and the cross. If the cross frame measures more than 620mm. long, it will have to be reinforced with thin wood supports, as the final weight of moss, flowers and foliage will make the design slightly springy. Place the supports on the frame, using two parallel ones or just one heavy one down the centre. Wire them firmly in place and then moss *over* these supports, so that when the design is finished, they are contained within the moss base.

No matter how small the cross frame is, it must be prepared with the utmost precision, so that the final outline is clear and firm. This means, in the first instance, that the four ends must be mossed very neatly. Begin at one of the ends and make sure that the moss is firmly attached, making a neat square end. This is not easy to do and will take a little time and patience to get perfect.

Work towards the centre of the cross, then turn the frame and begin at the opposite end and work towards the centre again. Most people find that they get a better finish to the four ends of the cross by beginning at the edge and working towards the centre, but if you prefer, there is no reason why you should not work right through both arms of the cross, thus making only two separate movements instead of four. Either way, the centre should have just a little extra moss so that it stands up slightly. This will give extra support to the central cluster of flowers.

Cushion, Pillow and Cushion Heart. These frames are bought in two parts, one being a flat base and the other a rounded top, between which you put the moss. The two pieces of frame are then anchored down with pieces of stub wire. The Pillow is long in shape – exactly like a pillow, in fact – whilst the Cushion is the same length on all four edges. The method of mossing is the same in each case. Bind moss on to the corners of the base first. Then tease out more moss and place it in the remainder of the frame. When you think there is enough, put the top on and wire it firmly in place. Remember that these designs, when finished, will have to carry quite a weight of wire, yet a solid design of this kind uses quite a surprising amount of moss. You have to try to preserve a happy balance between being too stingy with the moss, and making a base so thick and stodgy that it needs a crane to lift it! Only practice and experience will give you the right answer.

The Open Heart. In some districts this design is used more frequently than the Cushion Heart. The frame is mossed in the same way as a round wreath, but the shape must be kept very clearly. Where the frame narrows, the moss must be put on very carefully, otherwise it will lose its shape when finished.

Chaplet. This is a very pleasing design and is very popular in many districts. The frame is mossed, taking great care that the distinctive shape is preserved, and it may either be set with flowers all round with a special cluster at the wide base, or it can be based with good foliage with just a spray of flowers at the base. In some areas Cycas leaves are fixed to the long 'arms' and only the wide part of the frame is mossed, ready for a cluster of flowers and foliage.

These leaves come from the Cycas Palm and they are then treated so that they last almost indefinitely. They are very expensive and are available in two or three different sizes. The left-hand 'arm' of the Chaplet should have the Cycas leaf attached to it, first at the very top, then about halfway down and then, bending the leaf very gently to the shape of the frame, it should be firmly fixed at the base. The second leaf is then wired into place, so that the appearance at the top is of the right-hand leaf overlapping the left-hand one. The wide base of the frame is then mossed as usual.

Gates of Heaven and Broken Column. These designs are very popular in some areas, yet are never seen in others. They involve a great deal of work and are, therefore, always rather expensive. The mossing of the frame is most important. The wire frame should be turned upside-down so that the base can be filled with moss. Have a piece of wire mesh ready, cut to the same size as the base, and fix it in place to keep the moss in, when the design is stood up the right way. To make a really neat finish, some florists also like to add a finishing base made either of hardboard or heavy waterproof paper.

For the Gates of Heaven the remainder of the frame must be very carefully mossed, remembering that even when the flowers are added, the archway must still look delicate and slender.

The Broken Column is easier to prepare as you only have to fill the wire column with sufficient moss to hold the flowers. Check the tension of the moss with the designer because it is most essential that, when finished, the design shall be in the right proportion.

Vacant Chair, Harp. These are also special designs for which there may never be a demand in your district and yet which, in others, are quite usual. Check with the designer before you moss too much to make sure that it is satisfactory. It is surprisingly difficult to unravel moss from a design, so it is better to proceed slowly than to have to unpick it.

You may have a friend who is training to be a hairdresser, and no doubt she will tell you that for her first months she does almost nothing but shampooing and clearing-up! But this is just as important to the finished design as your work of mossing the frame is. It is a complete waste of time to set hair that has not been perfectly shampooed, and it is also very frustrating for a florist to try to work with a base that has been badly mossed. This is, therefore, one of the most important things you can learn. Only practice and an understanding of how the finished design should look will help you. Keep on asking questions, study all the designs you can and practice whenever you find yourself with a spare moment or so.

CHAPTER FOUR

Care and Conditioning of Flowers and Foliage

Flowers and foliage are the raw materials of the flower industry. Before they can be offered for sale they must be prepared and conditioned, so that they are looking their best. This may mean sale as cut flowers, or in funeral tributes, gifts, bouquets or vase designs.

Whatever they are needed for, the flowers and foliage must always be very carefully cared for when they arrive in the shop. Generally speaking, their first need is for a drink. If a freshly-cut stem is put immediately into water, it will usually drink easily. But if the stem is left to dry out, even for twenty minutes or so, a protective cover will form over the end of the stem and the flower will not be able to take in water.

When flowers are despatched from the nursery, unless they are transported direct to the shop in water in containers, the stems will dry out. Therefore, as a general rule, all stems should be cut before being stood in water.

First select a suitable container for the flowers. Never begin to unpack a box of flowers without having your vase all ready. If they are heavy-stemmed flowers, like Gladioli or Daffodils, remember to fill the container only half-way, as the thick stems will displace a good deal of water. More slender stems like Roses, Carnations or

Chrysanthemums will not displace nearly so much, so the container should be about two-thirds full of water.

Dry Pack. This is a comparatively new way of sending flowers to market. Usually when the flowers are cut they are given a long drink in deep water before being despatched. If they are sent dry pack it means that they do not have this drink and are packed just as they come off the plant.

There are numerous advantages in this type of packing. First, if the flower stems are full of water, the box will weigh more and will therefore cost more to send. Second, the goods will take up more space and fewer can be packed in one container. Third, if the stems and flowers are full of water, they are much more liable to bruising in transit. If they are completely limp they are less likely to snap off or to bruise. Although they do not look nearly so attractive in the box when packed completely dry, if they are properly conditioned they soon take in water and become ready for use.

Carnations. Most English-grown Carnations are packed in boxes of 36 or bunches of 20 like those from Holland which often have very long stems. They also come from Spain and South Africa and these bunches usually contain 20 blooms. Carnations drink very easily providing each stem is cut with a neat diagonal cut. If there are any leaves low down on the stem these should be stripped off. This, in fact, applies to all flowers, but take great care how you remove them. A stem which looks too bereft of foliage is not very attractive for sale.

The Carnations from South Africa and Spain often arrive very dry and in tight bud. The stems must be cut, as previously indicated, then stood in deep water and the flowers stored in a cool place until the flower begins to show its natural form.

When handling Carnations, remember that the flower is very heavy in relation to the stem. Always hold them with the flower downwards, otherwise the stems may snap or become entangled. Carnations, even when dry, are very brittle, so handle them with great care.

Roses. When time permits, the thorns should be trimmed from the whole stem. When it has been de-thorned, this obviously makes the Rose easier to handle. Also, when they are being offered for sale, if you take one stem out of the vase and they have not been de-thorned, you may find that they cling to one another, so that they all come out at once.

Although there are a number of devices on the market for stripping the thorns from Rose stems, one still has to trim the upper part by hand. This is best done with your knife. Holding the stem in the left hand, trim off the thorns from the lower six inches of stem. Then take hold of this piece and trim the thorns from the remainder of the stem, holding the knife parallel to the stem and almost 'stroking' it against the stem. Take care not to split it with the knife. This sounds a tedious and lengthy operation, but with a sharp knife and concentration it can be done quite quickly.

Roses drink less readily in winter than in summer. If one or two refuse to take in water, cut the stem again and stand as deep as possible, even right up to the flower. They usually drink fairly easily during the summer months and then the big problem is to prevent the buds from opening too quickly. Do not expose them any longer than necessary to strong light – this is one good reason for doing the de-thorning as rapidly as possible. They should be stored in a cool dark place, and if they are also wrapped in a cone of damp paper, this will delay opening.

Gladioli. Are usually packed in bunches of five, either tied or held together with rubber bands. Cut the tie and cut each stem separately with a good diagonal cut. This exposes a greater surface to the water than if you just cut straight across, and means that the flower will take up the water that much quicker. This applies, not only to Gladioli, but to all flowers that have to have their stems cut. Gladioli rarely refuse to drink, no matter what the season. In fact, it should be remembered that they drink a great deal, so before going home in the evening, check all vases, and particularly those containing Gladioli, to make sure there is sufficient water for the stems to continue drinking during the night. This is particularly important during warm weather, because the flowers will drink faster and there may also be a certain amount of evaporation.

Anemones. The English-grown flowers are usually packed in cardboard boxes with from 12 to 36 bunches in each. Those that come from France are packed dry and very tightly. Providing that each stem is cut, Anemones usually drink very easily. They respond quickly to strong light, so that only a few bunches should be placed on display at a time.

Iris. These are generally packed in bunches of five, sometimes with three different stem-lengths, so that the bunches lie flat and all the flowers are 'faced'. If the flowers are to be sold separately, it is a good idea to prepare three vases and grade flowers according to length of stem. If they are all put together in one container, the taller flowers may damage the shorter ones as they are taken from the vase. Moreover, the shorter stems may be kept back for designs, whilst the longer ones will be more acceptable for cut flower orders. Irises usually drink very readily, but the flowers are easily damaged, so take extra care when handling them.

Daffodils and Narcissus. Generally speaking, these drink very easily. Some florists prefer to cut the stem ends, but frequently it is not necessary and the flowers can be stood directly into deep water.

Freesia. There are many ways of packing and bunching Freesia for market. Some bunches arrive with damp cotton wool round the base of the stems. This must be removed, otherwise it looks untidy and unpleasant. Freesia takes in water very readily but the stem ends must still be cut. The florets are very crisp so handle the bunches with great care. If possible, stand them back to back in the vases. Make sure, also, that the lowest florets are not submerged in the water.

Lilac. Has very woody stems which must be crushed or snapped off before being stood in deep water. The imported Lilac arrives very dry and it is best to stand the stems in warm water, whilst leaving the flower heads still wrapped up for an hour or so. When the stem has taken up water, the flower can be unwrapped carefully and put on display. Lilac hates draught, so display the vase away from direct draught and the cold of the window.

Tulips. The end of each stem should be cut and the bunches stood in deep water. If the stems are curved, stand the bunches facing inwards in the container and leave in the dark for some hours. They will usually straighten up as they take up the water. If they refuse, wrap them gently in a paper tube and stand again in water. Remember that all flowers turn instinctively towards the light and tulips do this more readily than most.

Chrysanthemums. Each bloom is valuable and must therefore be handled with the greatest care. The slightest knock will shatter the flower, so concentrate very hard when unpacking or handling these lovely flowers. Most of them have a very woody stem. Some florists prefer to crush them, like the Lilac, but it is quicker and just as effective to snap a small piece off the end of each stem before standing it in water.

If the end is crushed with a hammer, it leaves two or three inches of shattered stem, which will pollute the water more rapidly. Furthermore, if the flowers are used for decoration, this shattered end will neither drive into the foam base, nor will it stay on a pinholder. The softer stems, particularly some varieties of Spray Chrysanthemum, may be cut if they are too pliable to snap easily.

Violets. Cut the stems, stand close together in a bowl of the right height and, if the weather is not very cold, the flowers should be sprayed. This will make them look luminous and very attractive. Violets drink to a certain extent through their flowers and the bunches may also be stored in the box for a few days, providing they are well-sprayed each day.

Hydrangea. May be treated in the same way as Violets, except that it is not necessary to stand it in water at all. Hydrangea, even in summer, has wonderful lasting quality, providing it is always well-sprayed. If by any chance a flower head should curl up, plunge it into deep clean water head first. This may seem drastic treatment, but the Hydrangea – as its name implies – is a lover of water, and rarely complains of having too much.

Mimosa. This often arrives packed in plastic bags. It may be left like this for two or three days in a cool, dark place without spoiling. If some is needed for display, the stems should be well-crushed and stood in hot, but not boiling water.

Foliage. This needs as much care as flowers. In some districts where foliage has to be transported long distances, it costs as much as, if not more than the flowers and should therefore have its full share of care and respect! The hardwood stems must be crushed with a hammer. Stand in deep containers full of water. Make sure that all stems are, in fact, plunged deep into the water. Generally speaking, foliage drinks easily, but it can only drink if all the stems ends are, actually, right in the water.

These are only some of the basic rules for the care of flowers and foliage. Each florist has his or her own favourite method of dealing with them, usually related to the source of supply. For instance, if all flowers are received direct from a grower and transported in water in containers, they need little or no conditioning on arrival. If, on the other hand, they have travelled in boxes, perhaps by air from the other side of the world, they need good care and attention before they can be used or offered for sale.

There is more than one way of conditioning flowers and foliage, but the general rule is – stem cutting or crushing, deep drinking and no draughts.

Plate 5 (*above*) An effective but simple-to-make table centrepiece. In the middle is a foam block around which polished fruit and laurel leaves are arranged. Lastly short-stemmed tulips are closely set into the block with the flower stems slightly longer towards the centre to create a gentle curve; *Plate 6* (*below*) The evaluation and judging of bridal bouquets in open competition is a matter for solemn concentration. A great deal about different concepts of design can be learnt from these competitions which are staged both nationally and internationally.

Plate 7 (left) This arrangement illustrates some of the basic principles of flower design. Notice the strong main perpendicular created with the long-stemmed iris (an extra turret of foam, firmly secured by a thin wooden stick to the main block of foam, is instrumental in achieving this effect).

Plate 8 (right) All-the-year-round chrysanthemum as a table centrepiece. This variety of chrysanthemum, having normally upwards of ten buds and open flowers on a stem, needs to be carefully trimmed for such an arrangement.

CHAPTER FIVE

Wiring, Mounting and Taping

Why do we wire flowers? Some people say they think it is a pity to impale flowers on wire and make them look unnatural. They could not be more right. It is not only a pity, it is clumsy and stupid to make any flower look stiff and unnatural, but it is just as stupid to allow beautiful blooms to be shattered for the want of a little discreet support and control.

This is why you must choose exactly the right gauge of wire to use and why the wire must always be as close to the flower stem as possible. This is nothing like so baffling as it sounds. In fact, the flowers themselves will give you a clue as to which wire is needed, and which method of wiring to use, if you study the shape of the bloom and the formation of the stem.

Flowers can be divided very roughly into three groups:

A. Those with a strong calyx, such as Rose or Carnation.
B. Flowers with a small calyx in relation to the size of the bloom, like the Chrysanthemum or Dahlia.
C. Flowers with little or no calyx, such as Tulip, Iris, Hyacinth or Orchid.

Stems, also, may be divided into three categories:

1. Woody stems, like Chrysanthemum, Rose or Carnation.

2. Hollow stems, such as the Daffodil or Anemone.
3. Semi-hollow stems, like the Tulip. Both Tulips and Carnations have very pronounced joints – or nodes – where the foliage joins the stem.

Method. A Carnation is probably the easiest flower on which to begin wiring practice. It has a good solid calyx and the bloom is not easily shattered. Take the wire,

Fig. 2.

gauge 0.90 or 0.71, in your right hand with the point aimed at the underneath of the calyx. The wire should be completely parallel to the flower stem. Support the flower head with your left hand and insert the wire firmly into the calyx. There is a seed pod within the flower and you will feel a slight check when the wire comes into contact with it. Twist the wire round the stem with your right hand, following through with the left hand, so that the wire is stroked very close to the stem. The word 'stroke' is used, rather than 'twist' because the wire must always lie very close to the stem, and it is your thumb that will do this, whilst your fingers support the stem from behind (Fig. 2).

Fig. 3.

Obviously, if you are left-handed, the whole process must be reversed, unless you are one of those lucky people who can work equally well with either hand.

Wire *Roses* by the same method remembering to try to persuade the supporting wire round the foliage. This is not easy but it is a pity to strip all the foliage off the stem through working too quickly or carelessly.

35

Chrysanthemums will also be wired in this way, except that it may be necessary to use a wire gauge 1.25 for better support. Unlike the Carnation, they do not have a nice firm seed pod to help you, so insert the wire very gently into the calyx and then pass it round the stem, taking care not to strip off too many leaves as you do so. As you twist the wire, it should lie more or less diagonal to the stem. Do not have too many twists, otherwise the whole thing will look like a corkscrew. On the other hand, if you do not have sufficient, you will not get enough support (Fig. 3).

All this probably sounds very complicated, but it is surprising how quickly and easily you will soon be able to do it. A good florist relies enormously on sense of touch, and as soon as your fingers become accustomed to the right amount of pressure you will begin to work quickly and surely. Do not get bothered because at first you seem to be working slowly. It is much better to begin carefully, to master these basic methods and then you will find that you soon gain speed and confidence.

As previously mentioned, Chrysanthemums, Roses and Carnations are listed under category 1, and the method of wiring just explained is known as *Exterior Wiring*. This is exactly what the name implies. Because the stems are either woody or solid, the wire support has to be applied to the outside.

Category 2 – Interior Wiring. When the flower has a hollow stem, it is usually possible to insert the wire either down or up through the centre of the stem, so that it is almost invisible. This is, of course, the ideal way of wiring, but only certain flowers are adaptable to this method.

Daffodils usually have a wide, hollow stem, but it narrows considerably just under the seedpod. Make a small hook in wire gauge 0.90 or 0.71, hold the stem firmly just below the flower head and insert the wire gently through the flower and down through the stem. Your left hand will feel the wire moving down the stem. Press the

Fig. 4.

hook gently down into the flower, by which time the other end of the wire has probably emerged from the bottom of the stem (Fig. 4).

If the flower has a particularly wide stem, you may find that it twists on the wire. Then it will be necessary to use Method 3, as follows:

Category 3 – *Semi-interior Wiring*. Although Tulips have hollow stems, where each leaf joins the main stem you will find a node. It is very difficult, in fact almost impossible, to drive a wire neatly past these joints, so you must therefore use a mixture of wiring methods both 1 and 2. Insert the wire into the stem just above the first node and

Fig. 5.

guide it gently upwards until it meets the seedpod inside the flower. Remembering that tulips are very brittle, bring both your hands to the spot where the wire first entered the stem, and holding this place firmly with your left hand, wire down on the outside, as you did with the Rose and Carnation (Fig. 5).

Use this method for wiring *Iris*, but you will have to insert the wire into the stem only two or three inches below the flower. The Iris has no firm seedpod in the centre, so take great care that the wire does not come out through the middle of the flower.

The majority of flowers in general use will fall into one of these three categories, but there are, of course, some exceptions. Lily-of-the-Valley, for instance. Although these flowers look so graceful, they are very brittle and one has to be extremely careful not to knock the delicate florets off the stem.

Use the finest wire available, gauge 0.20 is ideal. Leave an end of wire about 6omm. long and then begin winding up gently between the florets from the base of the flower stem towards the tip. When you reach the top flower or bud, wind the wire twice gently round the tiny stem and snip off very carefully with sharp scissors. This is a hollow-stemmed flower and the mounting wire can therefore be inserted right into the stem and then secured with the spare end of wire that you left at the base of the flower.

When the flowers are particularly robust, some people prefer not to wire at all. In this case, take a piece of damp cotton wool, lay it against the stem, lay the mounting wire on it, give it a twist or two and then seal with tape.

Referring back to the flower groups A, B and C, group A may also be wired by passing the wire *through* the calyx and drawing both legs of wire down parallel and close to the flower stem (Fig. 6).

Group B. This is a tricky group of flowers to wire. They will usually accept the method described in the previous paragraph, but spray Chrysanthemums, in particular, are apt to shatter. If this happens, use the hook method, as described for Daffodils, except that the wire will be usually on the outside of the stem.

Group C. One of the most-used flowers in this group is Freesia. Very popular flowers for both corsages and bouquets, they need the most careful treatment, being fragile and easily bruised. Buds and half-open flowers may

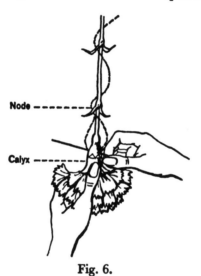

Fig. 6.

just be mounted by making a small hook in wire gauge 0.46 or 0.38, laying it against the floret and then twisting the long end twice round the hook and the throat of the flower itself. For wiring open flowers, the wire should be protected either with a small piece of damp cotton wool or be taped. This is how you do it:

Tape the top inch of wire gauge 0.46 or 0.38 and make it

into a neat hook. Insert into the Freesia flower, drawing the end of wire right down through the neck so that the hook rests neatly in the heart of the flower. This taped wire will keep the neck of the flower apart and will make a firm base on which to tape. If a bare wire is used, the fingers will crush the flower as the tape is put on, and the Freesia will fade more quickly (see Fig. 4).

If you prefer the cotton wool method, make a small hook in the wire, hook up a tiny piece of cotton wool and dip into clean water. Continue as described above.

Eucharis Lily. These beautiful blooms may be wired by the same method, except that being larger, you will need a little more cotton wool. Wind a small piece round the base of the flower before taping, as this will give the flower added support and longer life. When working with special flowers such as these, have a clean soft towel on the bench and lay the wired flowers on it. Never put these delicate blooms straight down on the workbench. Some florists prefer to insert their prepared flowers into a block of foam or a vase filled with moss. Whilst you will enjoy working near a heater, remember that the flowers should be kept as cool as possible.

Stephanotis and *Hyacinth*. These flowers are somewhat similar in shape and both are very popular for bouquets and corsages. Stephanotis usually has a very short stem and it is sometimes possible to insert a fine wire into the stem, up through the flower, make a tiny hook and draw it back firmly into the flower. If the stem will not take the wire, pass it gently through the base of the flower just above the calyx, then put another one through in the opposite direction and draw the two lots of two fine wires down parallel to the stem. Stephanotis is quite a robust flower but it is apt to part from its calyx rather easily. This is something you have to do your best to avoid, because without this tiny green base the flower is not nearly so attractive, nor is it so easy to model into the design.

Hyacinth may be wired with the Interior Hook Method if the stem is large enough to accept the wire. If not, use the Hook Method from the top of the flower, or pass a very fine wire through the base of the flower and draw the two ends down firmly together. Try at all times, however, to wire the flowers so that the wire is not easily seen.

Gardenia and Camellia. These are, perhaps, two of the most fragile flowers used by designers. They are usually packed on beds of cotton wool and some should always be handy to lay the blooms on after they have been wired. One cannot rely on the calyx for support and therefore they must either be supported with a little collarette of foliage or white paper, or both.

Method. Turn the flower upside-down and pass two wires gauge 0.46 or 0.38 through the base of the flower. Pull them carefully back parallel to the stem and fix by twisting one round the other three. Take a piece of medium-weight white paper and make a small hole in the centre, large enough to allow the stem to pass through. Work this very gently upwards towards the flower until finally it is resting against the outer petals. Turn the flower upwards and trim off the paper until it is invisible from the front yet be sure to leave sufficient to support the flower. This operation calls for a very steady hand and it is unlikely that a very junior florist would be asked to do it. Unfor-

Wiring, Mounting and Taping

tunately, florists are not able to use these beautiful
flowers very frequently and you might work for six months
and never see one, so that to know how to do it in theory
is, at least, one step towards understanding how to wire a
Gardenia or Camellia in actual practice. If you get an
opportunity, try the same method with a large Azalea
flower. They are very similar in shape and form, are just
as fragile, but happily, are not quite so expensive!

Mounting. This means the addition of an extra wire so
that the designer has more control over the flower. It is
most frequently used for funeral tributes when Carnations,
perhaps, are wired on 0.90 gauge, then mounted on 1.25
gauge wires to make a spray or cluster. The mount should
always be applied to the wired stem with a piece of
foliage. This saves both time and wire and, in the case of
funeral tributes, it helps to diminish weight.

Method. Make a hook in the wire, place selected piece
of foliage against base of wired stem, lay the hook against
the foliage and twist long leg of wire round very firmly.

Using much finer wires, one can also mount tiny
flowers into small clusters ready for putting into massed
designs. Violets, Hydrangea and the Narcissus known as
'paper white' are prepared in this way.

Next to mossing, probably one of your earliest jobs will
be to wire up the green ready for use in funeral tributes.
The one in most general use is a variety of Cupressus,
commonly known as 'flat'. This is a long-lasting evergreen
which can be cut and mounted into neat sprays and which
can be prepared and stored in a cool place ready for use.
Cut the branch neatly and as economically as possible
into sprays about 100mm. long. Try to cut down into a

43

node, so that there is a minimum of waste. If you just cut the branches straight across you are going to get a lot of very ugly and obviously 'barbered' ends (Fig. 7).

Arrange two or three pieces in the left hand, make a small loop with wire gauge 0.90. Lay loop on stems and hold very firmly between left-hand finger and thumb.

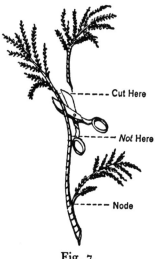

Cut Here

Not Here

Node

Fig. 7.

Twist long end of wire very tightly twice round and straighten the remaining piece, which should now measure about 100mm. long (Fig. 8).

A second method of mounting foliage is to bend the wire almost evenly in half. Twist the slightly longer leg round as in method one, then both legs will be the same length. The sprays of green can then be pinned into the base. This does not mean, however, that the wire may just be driven into the base as pins are put into a pin-cushion, because they would be likely to come adrift as soon as the design is handled. To be sure that they are firm, the wire must be driven in at an angle and the spray should then be bent back over the wire. The two wire legs thus form a kind of hairpin inside the moss base which should hold each spray firmly.

Taping. This is the final operation in the preparation of flowers and foliage for bouquets, etc. It must be as

Fig. 8.

discreet as the wiring, if the finished design is to look as good as possible. Floratape stretches easily and must be pulled hard in the right hand whilst the left hand rotates the wire between the finger and thumb. Practise with an ordinary wire in various gauges. You will find that the finer sizes are more difficult to tape neatly, and you must practise until you get a really smooth finish. For some

45

work the tape can be cut in half and this gives a much finer finish, as well as only using half as much tape.

Guttapercha does not stretch so much as Floratape, but it is thinner and generally makes a finer finish. It is not as adhesive as Floratape and some designers prefer to work with one kind of tape, whilst others do not mind which they use, so long as the colour is in keeping with the design and the finish is good.

It is always good to be able to work with a variety of materials – never get into a rut in flower design – or anything else, for that matter. Always be ready to try and to learn something new. Regardless of how experienced you ultimately become, there always *is* something new to learn. That is what makes floristry so fascinating.

CHAPTER SIX

Basic Design

It is most intriguing to look into the Oxford Dictionary and see the various meanings of the word 'design'. Two of the most forceful are 'mental plan' and 'scheme of attack'. It goes on to say 'to contrive, to plan, to intend'. We need all this, of course, in our flower shop and, indeed, in our everyday life. Without plan or intention, it is doubtful if we would ever get out of bed in the morning, let alone make a flower design.

We are, however, concerned with the bare meaning of the word 'design' which implies, in general, that everything that comes from the florist's workroom needs a good deal of thought.

Fortunately, however, the same rules of design apply, regardless of what you are making. For example, although an arrangement in a vase does not look very much like a bridal bouquet, it should be made according to the same basic formula.

There is a world of difference in size and appearance between a corsage and a funeral sheaf, but if you understand the rules for one design, you will be able to make the other, still using the same basic principles.

If you think of the five-finger exercises on the piano, which everyone has tried to play at some time or other, it is amazing how much real music an accomplished musician can produce using only those five notes. When he has learnt to play a scale, which, after all, is only a repetition of the eight notes of the octave, that is all he has in the way of raw material for making music. The flower designer is working with something much more tangible – with flowers and foliage of a multitude of shapes, sizes and colours with an immense variety of possibilities.

But unless these raw materials are understood and the basic principles of design are followed, a confusing muddle may emerge, rather like when a very young child goes mad on the piano keyboard.

The various points which add up to good design in floristry may be summarised as follows: 'Design' must first be sub-divided into two sections, the *visual* and the *technical*.

The visual is that which we see. The technical is the method of work which we follow to achieve the visual.

Design (*Visual*) = 1. Shape
2. Outline
3. Balance
4. Colour
5. Texture

1. *Shape* means the general impression of the design as a whole. For example, in relation to a vase arrangement, this would include not only the flowers and foliage, but the harmony of the materials in relation to the container. Shape may be further sub-divided into *profile* and *depth*. This is particularly important in designs which might be seen from any angle, for example, a bridal bouquet or a funeral tribute.

2. *Outline* implies something similar to a sketch plan. Whilst it would be difficult to explain 'depth' by drawing

it on paper, outline can easily be defined by a rough sketch. Good outline must be readily apparent at almost any reasonable distance. If, for example, one put a vase containing a few bud roses in a very large room, it might not be possible to see the detail of the design from one end of the room to the other. But if it had distinctive outline one could quickly register whether the design was, say, tall and slender, long and narrow or rounded.

3. *Balance* in its visual sense will be the outcome of a good outline, a pleasing shape, the correct and appealing use of colour and the right placing of the focal point. Balance encourages the eye to understand and appreciate the design, and to be able to travel comfortably from one point to another.

4. *Colour* must be defined at this stage as one of the most important tools of flower design. There are some people who say gaily 'all flowers grow, don't they, therefore all go together!' One might just as well say that because onions, ice cream and kippers are all food, they can be served up for dinner on the same plate. In fact, it is doubtful if they would even appear at the same meal together.

5. *Texture.* This is understood with fabrics in the difference in surface of, say, a length of green tweed and a length of green silk. Because each is a different fabric, the surface and the 'touch' is different. Texture differences in flowers and foliage are, perhaps, not quite so obvious as this example, but compare, for example, an Arum Lily with a Carnation, a Tulip with an Iris. Compare, also, the smooth silvery leaves of the Iris with the bright green crinkly leaves of Pittosporum. Think of the contrast

D   49

between Asparagus plumosus and Ivy foliage. All green, all **leaves**, yet all different shapes, colours and textures.

Design (*Technical*) = 1. Base
                       2. Vertical
                       3. Lateral
                       4. Focal Point
                       5. Balance, actual

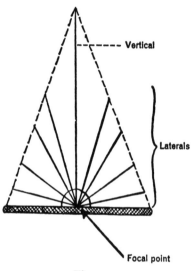

Fig. 9.

1. *Base* may be either a container or vase, or in the case of a funeral design, it will be the prepared shape, before the final cluster of flowers and foliage is put on.

2. *Vertical.* This will be your initial guiding line. It will probably be the first flower to be placed into the base, and should mark the highest point in the outline (Fig. 9).

3. *Lateral.* Having established your vertical, all other stems, wires or units that are worked in will come under this heading.

4. *Focal Point* forms the main point of interest in the design. It will be on or very near the spot where the vertical joins the base.

5. *Balance* is controlled by the proper placing of material. Actual balance is easier to define than to put into practice! It involves the correct preparation of the base, the correct choosing and placing of the material so that the finished design will stay in place.

Good design adds up to an understanding and practice of the basic rules, plus – and this is very important – plus a certain amount of personal inspiration and artistry. Then and only then will the design have personality and impact.

Have you ever noticed how one person can wear a dress and look quite nice in it, but no more than that? Another can wear one of similar colour and design and look really striking, usually because she has added some personal touch which underlines or illuminates the basic design with something of her own personality.

Some people imagine that one has to be endowed with all manner of artistic gifts to become a florist. Yet anyone capable of co-ordinating brain, eyes and hands should be able to master the basic technical requirements. But when you add imagination and an intense interest in the world in general, as well as the world of flowers, then you have a flower designer.

CHAPTER SEVEN

Vase and Bowl Designs

Designing flower arrangements on a commercial basis is very different from arranging the flowers at home. There you are probably working to please yourself, and if by chance a flower should slip out of position, you are probably handy to put it right. Anything that you make for display in the shop or for a client usually has to be designed to suit someone else's taste. It probably also has to be made to a specific price. And, of course, it must be firm enough in the container to stand being transported from place to place.

The container chosen must, of course, be sufficiently large for the flowers. On the other hand, it should not be so big as to make the flowers look lost in it. We have all seen the vase of three carnations and a wisp of fern on a restaurant table. How different those three flowers would look if they were cut down and placed in a very small container with a few well-chosen leaves, so that one could look down on the blooms instead of being face to face with three stalks!

There must always be harmony between the flowers and their container. This means that the finished design should look as natural as possible. Except in very rare instances, the flower design itself should be the work of art that arrests the eye, so that people say 'what a beautiful flower design', rather than 'what a lovely vase with flowers in'.

Mechanics. A fairly small container may be filled with a soaked block of foam, unless you are going to use daffodils or narcissus, which have stems which do not drive very readily into this preparation (Fig. 10). If only a few daffodils are going to be used, make a hole in the foam with another stem or piece of cane, and then the stem can be driven into it without any trouble.

A larger container will need a piece of foam large

Foam block

Fig. 10.

enough to hold all the flower stems, but not necessarily large enough completely to fill the vase. The foam base may be supplemented with mesh, this being especially useful for heavy stems; if possible wire the mesh down and attach it to some part of the container. It is frequently possible to cut this safety wire when the design has been finished, as then the weight of material will keep the mesh in place (Fig. 11).

As with so many other things, different designers have different ways of preparing containers for arrangements, but above all, the base must be completely firm and secure before you begin to place the flowers. It is sometimes a temptation to begin and hope that by putting in sufficient woody-stemmed foliage, it will hold everything firm. This rarely works out in practice and if your first vertical does not stand firm, go back and start again.

Can the foam stand up above the rim of the container? Yes, in some cases it can, but it depends a great deal on the size of the design and the flowers to be used. If, for

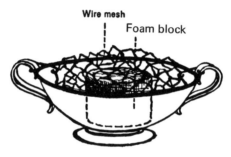

Fig. 11.

example, you are using heavy-stemmed flowers like Gladioli, or ones with heavy heads like Chrysanthemums, you can imagine that there is going to be quite a strain on the foam. Any stems that are put in at an angle approaching the horizontal are bound to be very 'head heavy' and they may eventually split the block across. If, however, wire mesh is used as well, this will, to a certain extent, take the weight. It is always helpful to have the wire mesh standing up in a kind of cone above the rim of the container, because it gives valuable support to the stems and helps you in the graceful placing of the laterals.

54

Vase and Bowl Designs

Outline. A simple flower arrangement usually looks more attractive if it follows a basic geometric design, such as a tall, slender triangle, or a shallow wide one. Draw the outline roughly on paper first and try to follow it with the flowers. As a general rule, use your pointed flowers to emphasise the outline and the rounder ones for filling in. If you look at a flower growing on the plant, you will notice that in most cases the stems rise up out of the foliage and also that, in many instances, the buds are at the top whilst the more mature flowers are lower down. The Gladiolus spike is a perfect example, not only of outline and shape, but also of colour and balance. The topmost buds are pale green whilst lower down the stem colour is just beginning to show. Lower still one or two flowers have opened which offers us a point of interest that arrests the attention.

The object of a flower arrangement is to give us something attractive to look at. When the design is good, the eye can travel gently from one point to another, from the top bud or flower, down to the centre of the design, then out again along one of the laterals to appreciate the line and balance of the arrangement.

If, however, shape, colour and balance are not in pleasing proportion, the eye will be forced to concentrate on too many points at once. This does not mean, of course, that all flower arrangements must be soothing. No one wants to listen to soft music all the time. A certain amount of 'beat' or challenging rhythm makes life interesting. It is quite possible to make a flower design both arresting and challenging without breaking any of the basic rules of good design.

55

Try, at first, with a simple 'faced' design. This means that the container will be placed against a wall so that only the front and sides are seen. Use two different flowers of contrasting shapes, say, Iris and Tulips or small Roses and Freesia. Having prepared your base put it almost on a level with your eyes. This may mean standing it up on something on the workbench, it may mean just taking your shoes off! Whichever way you arrange it try to have your eyes roughly at the same level as the focal point of the design.

After you have made a rough sketch of the design you hope to make, lay the flowers on the bench, following, as far as you can, your own plan. This will give you an idea of how and where to cut the stems. Place your first stem well back in the container, remembering that each flower must be seen to be enjoyed. Following your diagram, put in the laterals. Obviously these will not all be driven into precisely the same spot, but they must look as though they all 'belong' to the same focal point.

Use the natural foliage belonging to the flowers where possible. Use foliage to underline and complement the design and make sure that no leaf or branch of foliage spoils the clear effect of your outline (Fig. 12).

Even though you are making a faced design, the back should always bear inspection, so mask any mechanics still showing with a few carefully-placed pieces of foliage.

In the beginning, concentrate as much as possible on line. Work with not more than two different kinds of flowers. Practice with the same kind of flower in two different colours, say, two varieties of Tulip. Or take two different flowers in the same colour, perhaps yellow Roses and Carnations. See how the varying colours, shapes and textures affect your design. Take two identical bunches of flowers and arrange them in different ways in com-

Fig. 12.

pletely different containers. See what a surprising difference in design you achieve.

Study as many designs made by other people as you possibly can – in shop windows, in churches, at exhibitions and at home. Do you see 'a vase of flowers' or are you enjoying 'a Flower Design?'

CHAPTER EIGHT

Buttonholes and Simple Corsages

What do people expect when they order a buttonhole or corsage from the florist? Whatever their choice of flowers, one thing is certain. They want them to last well and to stand up to being worn or handled, perhaps in a very warm atmosphere. This adds up to three things – that the flowers chosen must be of the best possible quality, that they must have been well-conditioned before being used, and that they must be properly wired and finished.

Foliage forms an essential part of most designs, and it should be wired just as carefully as the flowers. Try to use the flower's natural leaves whenever possible. Asparagus plumosus still has its rightful place in design, but it is not used nearly so lavishly in corsages and bouquets as it was some years ago. Florists, generally, are much more imaginative in their use of foliage now and, providing a leaf will remain crisp and fresh, the choice is as wide as you choose to make it.

Wiring, General. When wiring flowers and foliage for designs to be either worn or carried, it is usual to take away most of the stem. This helps to diminish the weight and makes the finished design lighter and more delicate in appearance.

Wiring Foliage. Leaving about half an inch of stem attached to the leaf, stitch through the central vein with wire gauge 0.38 or 0.32. Draw both halves of wire down parallel, keeping the point where it pierces the leaf held firmly between left-hand finger and thumb. If you let the wire swivel about in these two tiny holes you may tear the fabric of the leaf and it will not stay fresh so long. For larger leaves, it may be necessary to support with three wires (Fig. 13).

Fig. 13.

For very special designs, the wire can first be taped for an inch or so and then fixed to the back of the leaf with sellotape. Make sure that the leaf and your hands are completely dry, otherwise the tape will not stick. The sellotape also gives the leaf extra support and it is particularly useful for bouquets that need larger foliage.

Leaves can be wired and taped ready for use two or three days before they are needed. They should be stored in small plastic bags sealed with an elastic band and kept in a cool dark place. Flowers, also, can be prepared and stored in the same way, which is very helpful when there is a lot of work to get through at the peak of the wedding season.

Carnation Buttonhole (Gentleman). Tape the centre of a wire gauge 0.71 x 180mm. This tape will hold the wire firmly in the calyx of the flower and prevent it from slipping. Drive the wire through the calyx as low down as

Fig. 14.

possible, draw the two ends tightly together and finish with tape. The wire 'stem' should measure about 90mm. when finished. If fern is wanted this should be mounted on a fine wire and placed behind the flower, then the wires are taped firmly together to make one stem (Fig. 14).

Carnation foliage makes a very neat finish to a formal buttonhole. Take three leaves, one slightly longer than the others. Stitch them with fine wire and tape all three together for about one inch, arranging the two shorter ones fanwise on the outside of the longer one. Place them behind the flower and finish with tape on one single stem.

For informal day wear, many gentlemen like a Clove Carnation. This is so called, because it has an aromatic fragrance like the perfume of a clove. It is wine-red in colour and is usually slightly smaller than other varieties, which makes it the perfect buttonhole flower. Clove Carnations may also be worn with a dinner jacket, but if the gentleman is wearing white tie and tails – for a very formal occasion – he should wear a white flower.

Before packing buttonholes for despatch, put a pin into each one so that they are ready for wear. They may be placed quite closely together and then sprayed, then seal the box ready for delivery.

Carnation Buttonhole (Lady). Prepare Carnation as before but tape the wire down to the end. Use either two or three pieces of asparagus or a few Ivy leaves. Tape each mounting wire to the end. Place the foliage round the flower, fix firmly in one place with fine wire and tape over very neatly. Trim the wire 'stems' neatly to varying lengths. If two flowers are wanted, wire each on gauge 0.71, length 260mm. Prepare four or five leaves, taping wires down to the end. Place Carnations with stems crossing, fix firmly with fine wire, adding foliage round the fixing point. Bind firmly with remainder of wire keeping this joining point as neat as possible, and then tape over. The corsage will have better balance and be easier to wear when the flowers are placed like this rather than with both stems pointing in the same direction (Fig. 15).

A more attractive way of making two Carnations into

a corsage is to shatter one and make tiny florets with the petals. Roll three or four petals gently together and mount on gauge 0.36 or 0.38. Tape these with the hook of wire facing you, so that the hook is rolled into the floret and becomes invisible.

Assembly – Rib or Unit Method. When making corsages and bouquets, one has to try to cut down weight as much

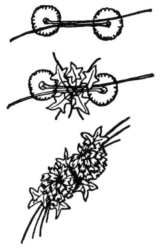

Fig. 15.

as possible. Mount several flowers or pieces of foliage on to one wire, so that the finished design is constructed with a number of 'units' instead of a multitude of small separate pieces.

A Carnation usually yields about nine florets. When these are ready wired and taped, take 4 wires gauge 0.56 x 180mm; tape three florets on to the first wire, taping the wire to the end. Then tape two florets on to each of the other three wires. You then have four units, one whole Carnation, plus four or five leaves.

Using the whole Carnation as your focal point, add the units to make a graceful design. Fix firmly with fine wire

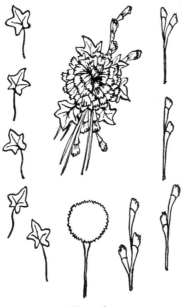

Fig. 16.

and tape over. Trim the taped 'stems' which should be arranged to give visual balance to the design. So that the stems do not look too bare and stark bend one flower unit and one or two of the leaves back over them. This is known as a 'returned end' (Fig. 16).

Most people prefer buttonholes and corsages not to be

63

too elaborate, so the florist must be careful not to design something which is too large and flamboyant for the client.

Rose Buttonholes. These are made in the same way as the Carnations, except that you add Rose foliage, and for a lady's buttonhole, perhaps also a few Ivy leaves for extra interest. For a gentleman, place one leaf at the back of the flower and two smaller ones in front. Tape the wires together making one neat slender stem.

For a lady, tape each wire separately, so that a Rose buttonhole with three leaves will, in fact, have four 'stems'. It is usual for a gentleman to put the flower stem either through his buttonhole or behind the coat lapel, but the lady will pin hers with the 'stems' showing.

Remember that any design, whether worn or carried as a bouquet, will be seen, not only from the front, but from both sides as well. This means that, although technically a 'faced' design, it must also have a certain depth, and must look just as attractive from the side as from the front.

Rose Pinning. This is usually done in hot weather or when the roses are being worn or carried in a hot atmosphere. Cut some tiny 'pins' about one inch long from wire gauge 0.32 and bend to form a hairpin. Holding the rose upside-down, very gently stroke one sepal down from the calyx and pin in position. Do this with each of the five sepals (Fig. 17).

This will hold the rose gently but firmly in position so that it does not expand any more. This must not, incidentally, be regarded as first-aid treatment for a rose which is past its best. Once it has really blown open, it will continue to move in spite of being pinned.

Plate 9 (above) A gift design for a wedding anniversary incorporating a hand-painted Japanese cup and saucer stuck together with a little adhesive. Nerine florets and Erica are based in a tiny foam ball attached to the saucer with tape. Although the foam should be well soaked, it is important that the saucer be completely dry as otherwise the tape will not stick; Plate 10 (below) Two blocks of foam fixed to a natural bark base and masked by moss are the basis for this free-style design demonstrating the French preference for mixing wild and cultivated material. White iris, short spray chrysanthemums and 2 stems of Singapore orchids make up the larger arrangement, while the smaller consists of a little iris foliage with a wild form of Cyperus gracilis.

Plate 11 (*above*) 'Classic' design entirely of Wedgewood iris. Notice how several of the left-hand laterals are cut longer than those on the right in order to avoid the visual boredom to which one-colour one-flower designs are prone; *Plate 12* (*below*) Discussion on taping a rose. The sepals have been pinned back to prevent the flower opening in the heat.

Neither is it a good idea to pin all roses regardless – this can result in a very stiff and artificial-looking design.

For a lady's corsage of two or three roses, choose a tight bud for the top flower. If possible, choose two other roses, one less open than the other. It is usually prudent to pin the most open one. The same applies to roses for bouquets and handsprays. Much of the appeal of the rose lies in its varying shape as it expands, so that it is usually

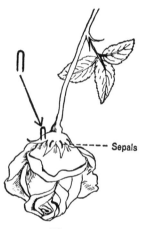

Sepals

Fig. 17.

only necessary to pin half of the flowers needed for the design.

It is best to do this as soon as the roses arrive from market, rather than waiting for them to begin expanding before being pinned.

Roses and Carnations are not, needless to say, the only flowers from which to make corsages. They may be designed with all foliage, with berries, in fact with any

65

growing material that has an interesting shape, form and colour and which will stand up to being wired and mounted. If you want to use something which has not been tested for lasting in your shop, wire a small piece, tape it and leave it lying on the bench for at least four hours. If it is still crisp then, you can be sure that it will be useful, but never use any material that you are not quite confident will last, because nothing looks more depressing than a corsage with some of its material already curling up.

Finally, spray your design and leave it ready for wear with at least two pins. If it is well-balanced, two ordinary dressmaker's pins will keep it in place and in the case of a single rose, one pin is all that is necessary.

CHAPTER NINE

Bridesmaids' Designs and Head-dresses

The designing and making of special corsages, head-dresses and flower novelties for bridesmaids is possibly one of the most interesting and rewarding branches of flower design. The work is, perhaps, the finest that the florist has to undertake as the finish and balance must always be quite perfect.

It is also especially exciting to create something that is attractive and which you know is for one particular person. It may be for someone of about your own age, in which case you would naturally take a very special interest. Or it might be for a very young bridesmaid. Tiny children, as you know, cannot be expected to concentrate for very long, and although they may walk demurely behind the bride, holding their flowers ever so carefully, the wedding ceremony probably seems as long as a lifetime to them.

They will begin to look for a diversion and will, of course, be very interested in their flower design and want to know, perhaps, exactly how it is made. If it has not been assembled very safely they may find out more about it than they are meant to!

One of the prettiest designs for a small bridesmaid is a baskette. This looks, when finished, just like a basket of flowers, but is much safer and easier to carry. Individual flowers and foliage are mounted in 'units' and are arranged in a tiny moss or foam base.

You must first decide how long the handle shall be. This, of course, depends on the height of the person carrying the design, and also on the size of flowers to be used. For example, if it is for a child attendant of, say, six years old, the handle need not be very long, otherwise the flowers will almost touch the ground. Obviously, the taller the person, the longer must be the handle.

Imagining that the design is for a six-year-old, take two wires gauge 0.90 and length 360mm. Tape them together starting 30mm. short of the tip and ending 30mm. short of the other end. Cover this taped handle very neatly with **narrow ribbon.**

Then with wire gauge 0.56 or 0.46, 90mm. long, make **tiny bows to match the ribbon handle. Net ribbon is the prettiest to use because it frills out easily. These bows** must be very tiny, not more than 60mm. across, and you will need about 15 of them. They are for finishing the underside of the design.

Next take a tiny ball of damp moss, just about the size of a large walnut, arrange it firmly and bind over two or three times with mossing wire, so that it stays in shape. Poke the untaped end of the handle through one side of the moss ball. Do the same with the other end and cross the two pieces of wire so that they lock together underneath the moss ball. The handle should then be quite firm. Make sure of this before you go any further with the design (Fig. 18).

Prepare units of flowers and foliage in varying lengths mounted on short wires, gauge 0.71 or 0.56. The gauge of the mount will, of course, depend on the weight of the flowers used, but try to keep everything as feather-light as possible. Since this design takes more flowers than one would imagine, make sure that you have enough before you begin to assemble the work. It is apt to spoil the line of the design if you are obliged to break off and make more units. If you find you have prepared too much material, you can always store it for at least 24 hours in a plastic bag and it might be useful for making a quick corsage.

Holding the moss base so that the handle goes from

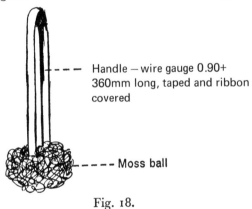

Handle — wire gauge 0.90+ 360mm long, taped and ribbon covered

Moss ball

Fig. 18.

back to front, not from left to right, begin to place your units, pushing the wire across the moss ball so that it comes out at the other side. Do not insert the wire from top to bottom if you can possibly help it, because it may spoil the finish of the base. Make sure, also, that all wires really are pushed safely back into the moss, because a sharp wire could prick a small hand and might cause tears at an unfortunate moment! When all the units have been arranged to form a graceful cascade effect, put in the

69

flowers which are to form the focal point. Make sure that no moss or bare wire is showing as you look down into the 'baskette' (Fig. 19).

All you need to do to finish it off is to put the net bows

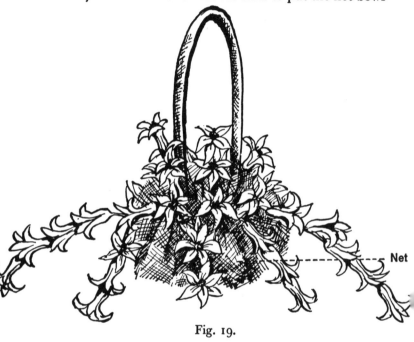

Fig. 19.

into the underside of the design, very closely so that no moss shows between. The wire mounts of these bows will need to be extremely short, probably not much more than one inch long. The flower units should be quite firm and the child attendant can then shake it about without doing any damage to the design.

Flower and Net Fan. As a change from the traditional

handspray, the older bridesmaids may like to carry tulle fans with a spray of flowers. These tulle bases may be bought ready made, but a very attractive design can be made in the workroom using ribbon bows to the client's particular choice. They are made of straight units built up of tiny bows and flowers placed alternately. They are comparatively easy to assemble, but they do take time, unless the bows are prepared well ahead. This, in fact, can be done, days and even weeks beforehand and the bows can be stored in plastic bags in a clean, dry place.

Take 7 wires gauge 0.90 and length 260 or 310mm. Tape them neatly from top to bottom. The bows should be mounted on silver wire gauge 0.38 or 0.32 and should be as tiny as possible. The number needed will depend on the size of the fan, but 5 on each rib makes a design which is usually large enough for the average bridesmaid. Therefore you will need 35 tiny bows and one or two larger ones to place at the focal point.

Next wire up small florets, perhaps hyacinth bells, violets, carole or garnet rosebuds, or something similar in size. Prepare 35 of these as well. Choose a few larger flowers to make a central spray, assembling it in the same way as if it is a corsage to be worn. The interest of this design is that the bows could even be made of the same material as the bridesmaid's gown, it can be made to any size and it can be finished with loops of ribbon making it look exciting and rather flamboyant. On the other hand, if the bride wants a very neat tailored design, you can use less ribbon and keep your corsage design very neat and even in shape.

You now have 35 tiny ribbon bows, 35 small florets, 2

larger bows and the corsage. Take the first taped wire and mount a bow on to the tip, then place a flower, then a bow and so on until you have mounted five bows and five flowers. As you tape in each item, you will find you have a little spare wire. Cut this off from time to time as it will diminish the weight of the finished design (Fig. 20).

Method of making ribbon or net bow

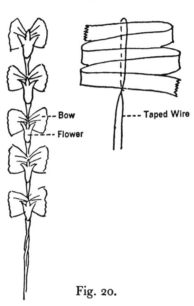

Bow
Flower
--- Taped Wire

Fig. 20.

Do this with each of the seven taped wires. Then place them together as shown in the diagram, fix them very firmly and tape the remainder of the wires together to form a small handle. If this seems too long, trim some off before taping. Measure it against your own hand. It should not show below the palm of your hand, but you must have enough to get hold of, otherwise it will be very tiring to hold (Fig. 21).

Add one larger bow to the front and one to the back at the focal point where the seven wires are joined together. Fix the corsage to the front with a taped wire. This design, being completely flat one side, is very easy to pack and transport and looks extremely pretty when finished.

Head-dress. The same principles apply in making a

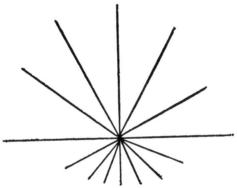

Fig. 21. Plan of Assembly for Fan.

design to be worn in the hair – the finish must be impeccable, especially when it is going to be worn by a very young person. Flowers and foliage should be carefully wired and each piece taped for about one inch only. Like the baskette, head-dress designs invariably take more material than one would imagine.

There are numerous ways of assembling a head-dress and one of the simplest is to work towards each end from the central flower. Take a wire gauge 0.90 or 0.71 and length in accordance with the required length of the design. Tape this wire from end to end. This will prevent the flowers and foliage from twisting round as it is mounted on.

Mark the centre of the wire and place your central flower. Then add flowers and foliage, gently bending the wire as you work to the shape it will be when finished. Trim off all wire that is not required, as it is essential that a head-dress is as light as possible. When you get to within one inch of the end of the foundation wire, make a returned end with a flower and a tiny leaf or two. Turn the design round the other way and work in the same manner outwards from the centre (Fig. 22).

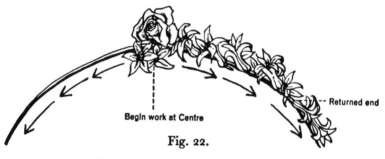

Begin work at Centre

Returned end

Fig. 22.

It is usually quite a help to arrange the flowers and foliage on the bench just as you intend to mount them on to the foundation wire. If you do not place them like this at first, it may be quite difficult for you to get both sides alike.

Head-dresses may be gently placed over a mound of soft paper for despatch. It would be an added service to the client to include a card of hair-grips with the order.

Tiny children sometimes have hair that is too fine to support hair-grips. But their flower head-dresses can be fixed another way which is quite safe. When you have taped the foundation wire, make a tiny loop each end.

Fix a length of fine hat elastic through these loops. This can then be passed underneath the child's hair and only one grip at the centre of the design will be needed.

So much of the weight of a busy wedding week-end can be taken off the last day by a little thought and preparation beforehand. Make sure that you have a stock of bows ready. These will, of course, have to be prepared with reference to the wedding orders, so store each set in a separate plastic bag with the name of the bride on the outside. If head-dresses are ordered, check that there are some cards of hair-grips in stock, also a yard or so of the fine elastic. If you are not quite so busy at the beginning of the week, these tiny items take very little time, but if they have to be taken care of at the last moment, they can completely upset an already tight schedule.

If you feel capable of being responsible for these items, suggest to your employer that you take this over. Do check, however, that everything is satisfactory. For example, show him the ribbon you plan to use for each wedding, show him a bow before you make the whole lot, making sure that it is the right size. If your handwriting is neat and clear, offer to write the labels for each wedding. Find out how your employer likes his boxes lined and prepared for the buttonholes and bouquets and look after this for him. If there is room to store the boxes, they can also, of course, be got ready well beforehand. There are so many ways in which the student florist can contribute to the general smooth running of the shop. Particularly by taking care of such small items mentioned above, in themselves not apparently especially important, yet each one adding up to efficiency and a smoothly-running workroom.

CHAPTER TEN

Funeral Tributes

This country generally gets rather more than its share of wind and rain so our funeral tributes must be designed with this in mind. Because, also, our funeral customs dictate that tributes are delivered either to the house of mourning or to the funeral director's office, then loaded on to following cars, then unloaded for the actual ceremony, they must be constructed to stand up well to rather a lot of handling.

However, this does not mean that each design has to be stiff and solid. Design and balance are just as important as with more delicate designs. Remember, also, that while the florist is quite accustomed to handling damp material, other people might not find this very pleasant, so a funeral tribute should be just as carefully finished as any other design that comes out of the workroom. One of the greatest menaces can be a sharp end of wire that has accidentally been overlooked. This could tear someone's fingers and cause both annoyance and inconvenience, so when you have finished your design, always check it for 'handling comfort'.

Sheaf. When finished, this should look like a natural tied bunch, but it should still have good line and design. The flowers can be wired where necessary for support, so that it can be easily handled without risk of damage. The sheaf is constructed in exactly the same way as a corsage, believe it or not! Following the 'constant vertical' rule, you need to select a strong, straight piece of foliage for a backing. Just as you no doubt choose the straightest and strongest stem for your first flower in a vase design, it is worth spending a little time on the selection of your first piece of foliage and the flower to begin the sheaf. At first you will probably find it easier to use not more than two

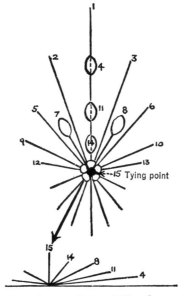

Fig. 23. Formal Sheaf.

kinds of flower, but as you become more expert you will, of course, have more variety.

When putting flowers into a container you have, of course, a visible base, but when making a sheaf your base is, in fact, your hand. You will be holding the design with your left hand as it gradually builds up and this tying point

77

should also form the centre of balance.

You will, presumably, be working with a limited amount of material, so you must plan how much you can spare for the main part of the design, which flower will emphasise the focal point, and how much material you have to spare for your 'returned end'.

Each flower stem and piece of foliage must be bound in separately, with one – or at most two – twists of the string. You must try to pull the string really tight. In fact, after about an hour of practice, you may find that the string has cut your finger. This does not mean that you are going to suffer for the rest of your career as a florist. You will soon find out how to get a firm finish without damaging your fingers, but if each piece of material is not fixed very firmly into place, it may shift and your design could come unstuck (Fig. 23).

Although you will find it most convenient to keep the design lying on the bench as you work, do not forget the back. It must also be very neat, so add more foliage as you work in the flowers, making sure that the finished design will lie completely flat. A tribute that rolls from side to side, or that rocks gently with the movement of the funeral car is not very attractive.

For a simple sheaf, the flowers and foliage may be worked in until only three flowers remain. These can, if necessary, be mounted with foliage and wired through the tying point. This will give extra elevation, dignity and interest to the finished design.

If any wires have been left below the tying point, they must be unwound from the stems and cut off neatly. Some florists like to bind all stems together and then cover with cellophane, but it gives the sheaf a more natural and balanced appearance if they are left separated exactly, in fact, like a natural bunch (Fig. 24).

The tying point can be finished with ribbon, foliage or cellophane ribbon, according to the value of the design. Make sure that no wires are left here to damage fingers.

Natural Stems

Fig. 24. Informal Sheaf. Flowers grouped to achieve maximum effect with minimum material.

For a large sheaf, construct as previously indicated, and when about half of the material has been used, add a small ball of damp moss to the tying point. This can be bound on with the string already being used. It will help to give extra support to the flowers that are to be mounted in.

Although the sheaf should, when finished, look as natural as possible, it must still have good design, which means that it needs to be well-planned. Assess the amount of material you have available, and if necessary, place it on the bench in position before you begin work, so that you get a rough idea of how it will work out.

An *Unwired Sheaf* is assembled in the same way, but the material must be chosen with extra care. You will not be able to rely on any wire support, so the flowers have to be selected, wherever possible, with good strong stems. This does not mean that they must all be completely stiff and straight, but if a stem does have a curve, make sure you use it to help your design, rather than trying to force it to go the opposite way.

Since an unwired sheaf is likely to be somewhat flatter than a sheaf, you can obtain some support and elevation after you have bound in the first few flowers by adding a small piece of moss to the tying point. The first piece must be quite tiny – about the size of a walnut – and then add more small pieces as you work in the flowers. Continue like this until there is sufficient elevation, adding foliage as well to hide the moss. An unwired sheaf is probably one of the most difficult designs to make, but because of public demand, it becomes a most necessary part of the florist's programme.

Set Designs. This involves preparing a base of flowers, usually of one colour, set or 'blocked' into the moss all at the same height. One needs patience and a very true eye, because it is most essential that the outline is precise.

For cushions, pillows, wreaths and other solid designs, the edge must be especially firm. The 'filling' flowers can usually be wired on gauge 0.71, but it is better to wire the edging flowers with a slightly heavier gauge to be certain

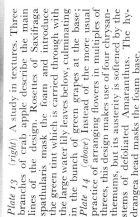

Plate 15 (above) A simple design for a buffet supper. The picture illustrates one of a pair of Indian candlesticks with the plastic pin holder attached. Wire mesh secured with tape makes a firm basis for the ten pink tulips and do remember to add more water after finishing the design as tulips need to drink continually.

Plate 13 (right) A study in textures. Three branches of crab apple describe the main lines of the design. Rosettes of Saxifraga spathularis mask the foam and introduce the green tint which is carried through with the large water lily leaves below, culminating in the bunch of green grapes at the base.

Plate 14 (above) Instead of the more usual practice of arranging flowers in multiples of threes, this design makes use of four chrysanthemums, but its austerity is softened by the stems of defoliated Amaranthus. The hydrangea head masks the foam base.

Plate 16 A flower hat is a fun thing to make and wear and also allows one to wear a new hat for every occasion. Dr Verhage rose petals were glued quickly to a hat base and a spray of buds, foliage and an open rose were attached to make this lovely wedding number.

of a completely firm finish.

For blocked bases, some florists prefer the pinning method, as described for green foliage base, whilst other designers wire right through and then return the remaining end of wire into the moss. Either method can be used, providing, in the first instance, that the pinning is absolutely safe and firm. In the case of the second method, the base of the tribute should not become a confused and untidy mass of wire loops. To avoid this, wires should be passed diagonally through the base and secured at the side of the tribute. This is not possible, of course, in the case of cushion designs, but if each wire is driven back into the base very firmly, it will bed in and not get in anyone's way. It is usual to finish set designs with a spray of special flowers. This is planned in the same way as the sheaf, following the same rules of design, but each flower will be mounted with a small piece of foliage and wired in independently.

If there is a shortage of flower material, it is quite permissible to add false stems to the spray, so that it looks, in fact, just like a natural bunch laid on to the flower base. This can be very attractive when Spring flowers are used, as they have such fresh-looking pale green stems.

Sympathy Basket. This is a design which is now in great demand in some areas. The container must have a solid flat base and the handle should be sufficiently high for the design to be easily picked up. Unless the client particularly asks for a 'faced' design, it is usual to make a shallow, slender arrangement, that, like the sheaf, looks attractive from all angles. The flowers should be based either in damp foam or moss. Never, needless to say, just wire mesh with water in the container!

Working into the centre of the basket, arrange the flowers and foliage in much the same way as for a sheaf, except that this will usually be done both ends of the basket. This design takes, of course, considerably more material than a small sheaf, but they are very attractive and clients choose them when they want something a

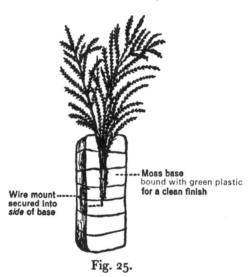

Wire mount secured into *side* of base

Moss base
bound with green plastic
for a clean finish

Fig. 25.

little more unusual and dignified. This design has the natural appearance of a tied sheaf, none of the flowers needs to be wired, yet it can be very easily handled and moved from place to place.

Funeral Spray. The finished appearance is similar to a sheaf, but the method of construction is different. Instead of being bound together, the material is mounted into a mossed base. In some areas, this is a flat bar, whilst in others it has a small support that forms a kind of easel which elevates the spray, adding to its attractive appearance.

The flowers and foliage must be wired and mounted at varying lengths to correspond with the shape of a sheaf. This design may be made either single or double-ended, or false stems may be added, according to the amount of material available. It is most important, however, that the mounting wires are secured at the side of this design. If they are driven through to the back the extra wire may cause the spray to rock (Fig. 25).

CHAPTER ELEVEN

Care and Maintenance of Foliage and Flowering Plants

Foliage and flowering plants usually form quite a large part of the display in many flower shops. Like the cut flowers, plants should always look fresh and attractive. They need constant care and attention, but on the other hand, they must not be killed with kindness.

The plants must not only look really healthy, but you should be able to give the customers some idea of how to care for them and keep them looking this way after purchase.

There are, certainly, many leaflets, care cards and whole books written on the care of plants, but customers still appreciate the personal touch as well. If you understand the plants, and if you have also helped to maintain and care for them, then you will be able to talk about them with a certain amount of authority and interest.

General. Plants, like people, usually prefer to live in reasonable comfort, with regular water and food. There are certain general rules of care and maintenance that apply to the majority of plants. Others, of course, have more specific needs.

They prefer an even temperature and, like most human beings, they detest a draught or a sudden change in temperature, either up or down. Plants need light, but during the coldest winter months it is not a good idea to

84

leave them on a window-sill, as the cold will be quite severe near to the glass, even if the room is centrally heated. It is better at this time to sacrifice a little light and keep the plants away from the windows, unless, of course, it is a house with double glazing.

Watering. Customers usually ask how much water a plant needs. This is very difficult to explain because it depends mainly on the temperature of the room. Even during winter, at the minimum growing season, if the room is really warm, then there will be quite a lot of evaporation and the plant will need watering more frequently than if it is kept in a cooler atmosphere. But plants must never be allowed to 'paddle'. That is to say, they need a good watering, so that all the soil in the pot is well-soaked, but the pot must not stand in the remainder of the water.

It is better to give a plant a really good watering only twice a week than to give it about a teaspoonful every day. It is very sad to see a plant that has had this sort of treatment. The top soil is quite damp and soggy but underneath it is bone dry and this is useless for the comfort and well-being of the plant.

Feeding. You will probably be amazed at the size of some of the plants in relation to the size of the pot in which they are growing. They do not need nearly as large a pot as one would imagine, providing they have a regular feed. This is most readily given in one of the brand-name soluble feeds. From the end of March through to the end of September, you can give this feed once a week, or once each two weeks, but do be sure that you follow the directions. If you put too much feed in the water it will scorch and eventually kill the plant.

Names. At first the names of the foliage plants may seem rather baffling. Some of them are long and apparently involved and you may feel that you will never remember them, let alone remember which plant they belong to!

Fig. 26. Hedera Canariensis.

If, however, you divide them into families, which is, after all, the way in which all plants are named, you will then only have to remember – so to speak – their Christian names. It is really no more difficult than getting to know a crowd of new people at a party.

The Ivy group is called Hedera. The lovely graceful plant with large leaves, part green and part pale yellow is known as Hedera canariensis (Fig. 26). The variety with small dark green leaves is called Hedera helix chicago. Most of these plants are clearly labelled and it does not take long to grasp the names, when you are

Fig. 27. Philodendron Scandens.

handling the plants every day. Notice that, unlike people, only the family name carries a capital letter. The Christian name – or variety – is written with a small letter, namely *h*elix *c*hicago.

Another very popular room plant is Philodendron scandens. This is a climbing or trailing plant with large heart-shaped dark green leaves (Fig. 27). Its cousin,

Philodendron monstera deliciosa looks very different, but it is just as popular, particularly with people who have large rooms. This variety is very large and impressive and grows fairly quickly.

Scindapsus 'Marble Queen' has the same shaped leaves as Philodendron scandens, but it is a much smaller plant with very unusual pale green and creamy-grey foliage. The stem is almost white and the foliage is very beautiful for special corsages and bridal bouquets.

The Peperomia family gives us a variety of shapes, sizes and colours in foliage. The leaves last very well when wired up for use in designs. Peperomia caperata has small dark green ribbed leaves, looking almost like thick velvet. This plant carries numbers of long white flowers, but it is almost as attractive without them. Peperomia sandersii has larger leaves with very distinctive marking and some-times a silver sheen, whilst Peperomia scandens is a very graceful trailing variety with pale green heart-shaped foliage edged with pale lemon. None of the Peperomias grows very fast, but they are very beautiful for using in arrangements with plants of darker foliage.

Tradescantia is, possibly, one of the easiest ornamental plants both to keep and to propagate. There are a number of varieties on general sale and, although the plant holds its foliage throughout the year, the leaves look decidedly more attractive during the warmer months. It prefers to trail rather than climb and it is very useful for corsages and bouquets. The leaves may be wired separately, or the tips of the trails may be used complete. If you put one of these tips in water it will put out roots in a matter of days.

The Begonia Rex, as its name implies, is a truly regal

plant (Fig. 28). There is a vast number of members of this splendid family and the interest is almost entirely in the beauty of the foliage. The leaves of most of them have a delightful habit of 'facing', that is to say, they bend towards the light, so that the whole surface is on view and the plant appears to be one mass of extravagant rich shape and colour. One must be careful not to allow the tips of

Fig. 28. Begonia Rex.

any leaf to touch the bench or display surface, as they will eventually bruise and turn brown.

It is inevitable with all plants, that during the growing season, new leaves will develop and old ones will shrivel and turn brown. The plant does not like to be cluttered up with these old leaves. Trim them out regularly and the plant will respond by always looking neat and tidy and in the best of health.

For a decorative plant, the Aphelandra is in a class by

itself (Fig. 29). With its large shiny green foliage, boldly striped with yellow, and pagoda-shaped bright yellow flowers, it is a plant full of personality. The flowers last for a number of weeks, but the plant is just as decorative, whether it is in bloom or not.

It needs more water than many room plants, and if it gets the slightest bit dry, the leaves will become limp. All

Fig. 29. Aphelandra.

plants with large leaves benefit by having their leaves wiped with a clean damp cloth from time to time. There is, unfortunately, always a certain amount of dirt deposit in the air, particularly in large towns. If the leaf gets too coated with dust and dirt, it cannot breathe properly. If a customer should ask you whether you advise cleaning the foliage with a sponge dipped in milk, the answer is definitely 'no'. The milk will form a coating of grease over the tiny breathing holes of the leaf. There are one or two preparations available with which one can clean the leaves and which make them look shiny and attractive.

The various lovely flowering plants now available are mostly reasonably tolerant of average living-room conditions. The same rules of care and maintenance apply as for foliage plants. That is to say, regular watering, even temperatures and an absence of draughts. Some clients, unfortunately, seem under the impression that both cut flowers and plants last much longer if kept in the coldest possible conditions! During some months of the year, when an unused room can be exceptionally cold, people have been known to put a gift of Chrysanthemums or perhaps a growing plant in this room so that 'it will last longer'. After a week they peep into the room and find that the flowers have completely curled up with cold. How much better to have them in the living-room and enjoy them at their best.

Most ornamental foliage plants are available all the year round, but flowering plants come, within a little, according to their proper season. The table below gives roughly the seasons of the various flowering plants available. Bear in mind, however, that supplies may vary from area to area, particularly where plants are bought in direct from a local nursery.

November, December, January

Azalea, Cyclamen, Heather, Chrysanthemum, Poinsettia, Primula obconica, Primula malacoides, Kalanchoe, Begonia Lorraine, Aphelandra.

February, March, April
Azalea, Chrysanthemum, Hyacinth, Tulip, Daffodil, Narcissus, Iris reticulata, Cineraria, Calceolaria.

May, June, July
Astilbe (Spiraea), Chrysanthemum, Hydrangea, Crassula, Pelargonium, Aphelandra.

August, September, October
Chrysanthemum, Primula obconica, Hydrangea, Cyclamen, Aphelandra.

CHAPTER TWELVE

Colour

You may wonder why on earth such an important subject as Colour has been left to one of the last chapters. In fact, it really needs a whole book to itself, particularly in relation to flower design.

Colour harmony is, perhaps, almost as personal a thing as musical harmony. Some people like a bright major combination of notes, whilst others prefer their music in a gentle minor key. With colour harmony, some people like strong, positive colours, whilst others prefer something a little more subdued. Colour is possibly one of the most fascinating basics of the universe when one thinks of it in relation to human behaviour. Think of a winter day, a grey sky, bare twigs on the trees, very little light and, of course, no sunshine. Now, if your imagination will stretch this far, conjure up your favourite summer scene. A bright blue sky, strong sunshine lighting up corners and casting interesting shadows through the trees, flowers in bloom and, of course, everyone wearing bright, gay summer clothes.

It is small wonder that many animals hibernate throughout the winter. With the lack of light and warmth, they have little natural incentive to bustle about their daily business of finding food. Human beings have to create for themselves an impression of summer comfort during the English winter by having stronger light in homes and offices, artificial warmth, even different types of food and drink from what they would choose for a hot summer day. In recent years it has been realised that colour has a remarkable effect on human behaviour and thus people who want to feel warm and cheerful during the greyest of winter days will choose bright, glowing colours for their clothes. The same people will probably wear cooler-looking colours during high summer.

Although we are getting many cut flowers out of their natural season, it is interesting to reflect that flowers in their right season seem, in general, to follow basic colour rules. Think of the numbers of bright yellow flowers we have in the Spring, the daffodils, tulips, freesia, crocus and primroses. Many of these flowers are in bloom in their natural state long before the leaves are on the trees. In fact, probably the earliest to come into bloom is the beautiful shrub called Hamamelis mollis; its bright yellow flowers uncurl on completely bare twigs early in January. Try to imagine how it would look if all these flowers, instead of being yellow, were blue or pink. They would not have nearly as much positive impact.

Yet advancing into summer we find that we have comparatively few yellow flowers. The delphiniums, lupins and larkspur, as well as hydrangeas, are mainly in the pink, blue, mauve range of colours. True, there are quite a number of yellow roses, but there are many more in the pink, orange and red colour range.

Autumn brings still warmer colours and even the flowers themselves seem more solid. Nothing could be much more solid or full of rich colour than a Chrysanthemum or a Dahlia. And in late Autumn berries are beginning to appear. Although there are, of course, some exceptions, most berries are deep yellow, orange or red. The Holly berry is, perhaps, the very essence of winter.

There is a very useful booklet on Colour and also a colour wheel available through the Society of Floristry. But it will no doubt be useful to have your own colour wheel handy. You can fill in the colours with either good crayon or paint. If you are using crayon, remember to

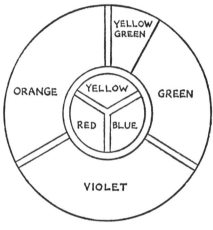

Fig. 30.

put a sheet of thin paper over the illustration when you have added the colour, otherwise the crayon may rub off on the opposite page.

Colour the space indicated with a clear, strong red. Clean the paintbrush thoroughly and then paint into the appropriate space a clean, powerful blue. Then do the same with yellow. Be sure not to fill in the narrow space between the colour divisions. Leave these white for the moment, and if you are using paint, make sure that each colour is perfectly dry before you go on to applying the next one.

When the red, blue and yellow has been filled in, you have the three primary colours. Now you can begin to make the secondary colours. Mix your original yellow and red in equal quantities and fill in the resultant *orange* in the appropriate space. Cleaning your brush and palette each time so that you are working with absolutely clean material, mix yellow and blue in equal quantities and put the *green* in its place. Lastly mix the blue and red and you find you will have a rich *violet*.

If you have ever seen a rainbow you will realise that it is composed of these six colours – red, orange, yellow, green, blue and violet. That is to say, the three primary colours plus the three secondary colours which, as you have already proved, are a mixture of a given two of the primary colours.

Having established these six colours, you can then begin to experiment. Take your basic yellow and add just a dash of blue. It will spoil the clear tint, but on the other hand, there will not be enough blue in the mixture to make a true green. This is what is known as a yellow-green. You can, of course, do this with each colour, getting some delightful variations in colour value.

When the six colours on the wheel are completely dry, take a very fine brush or pen and fill in the margin between half of them with black. Leave the remainder of the margins white or fill in with white paint. You will see that the colours that are divided by the black line appear much stronger than those divided by white.

Whilst you still have your paints handy, make another interesting experiment. Take a sheet of white paper and put a tiny dot of scarlet in the centre. Move a few paces away from the paper and stare at it intently for a moment or so. Then look away. You will still be seeing spots, not red ones as you might imagine, but green. This is the eye's instinctive protection against being 'bored' with too much red. Glance again at the colour wheel and you will notice that green is opposite red on the wheel. These two colours are known as 'complementary' to one another. Choose any colour and the one that is directly opposite on the colour wheel becomes the complementary of the first one.

Flower designs in complementary colour harmony are usually strong and arresting. Translating this into terms of floristry, a branch of well-berried holly, with the strong red of the berry clusters and glistening green of the foliage makes one of the most obvious complementary colour harmonies. A funeral tribute based with violets and with a spray of, perhaps, yellow freesia and yellow carnations is another striking example of complementary colour harmony.

Should you want something really discreet and under-stated, you might choose to make a design of all one colour, possibly pink carnations and roses. If, however, you use only one variety of carnation the design might look rather boring from the colour point of view. But if you blended two or three different varieties of pink carnation, this would probably have a very pleasing effect. Your colour harmony in this design, being composed of only one colour, is termed Monochromatic.

On the other hand, if you wanted to create a design with a little more impact, you might choose flowers in the yellow-orange range. Pale yellow tulips, deep yellow freesia and a few orange tulips. This combination consists of one primary colour (yellow) plus a group of colours nearby on the circle, but not trespassing into the orbit of a second primary colour. This third group is known as analogous colour harmony.

Most of us are far more aware of colour than perhaps we realise. There is considerable research going on into the effect of colour on human behaviour. Top business men sometimes call in colour experts to advise them on the interior decoration of their offices. It seems that certain combinations of colour will inspire confidence, some colours may help people to work more efficiently and others have a tranquillising effect on people. Hospitals, in particular, seek advice to find which colour scheme is thought to be the most restful for patients.

And not only human beings are affected by colour. It is said that a particular racing stable was having trouble with the horses which were kept in stables painted in dark red. Each time the horses were exercised or raced, they took a very long time to settle down again, and moreover, the stables were infested with flies which, naturally, irritated and further excited the animals.

An expert on colour was called in who advised that the stables be painted in pale blue. The horses quietened down in much less time and the flies were also considerably reduced. It would seem from this that neither flies nor horses like red very much, and, if one is to believe what one hears, neither do bulls!

98

Colour

The following table of colour symbolism is interesting:

Yellow signifies Light and Knowledge
Blue   ,,   Faith and Meekness
Orange   ,,   Pride and Self-respect
Red   ,,   Power
Green   ,,   Sympathy and Compassion
Violet   ,,   Piety
White   ,,   Purity and the essence of light

The following table gives a rough guide to the amount of one colour to use in relation to another. This is worked out on the power of impact of a given colour relative to grey. Thus:

$$Yellow = 3$$
$$Red = 6$$
$$Blue = 8$$
$$Orange = 4$$
$$Violet = 9$$
$$Green = 6$$

Keeping these two tables in mind, try sometimes to visit one or two of our art galleries. Study the paintings and apply what you already know of colour value to see if you can understand why the artist has used any particular colour in his work.

Colour, incidentally, has a marked appeal in food and the accomplished chef will always plan a menu with, not only an appeal of taste, but also a visual appeal based mainly on colour and shape. Visualise a plate with a piece of fresh salmon with a trimming of green peas – the perfect complementary colour harmony. One student had evidently mastered the basic rules of colour very well because when he was asked what he had for lunch, he replied 'monochromatic colour harmony – fish and chips!'

To summarize, florists possibly have more of a problem with the use of colour than most artists, because they are working with predetermined shapes, textures and colours, which cannot be mixed and blended at will like colours on the artist's palette. Neither can they resort to some of the dramatic lighting used in the theatre which can change the colour of a complete scene and thus basically change its impact. But there is no doubt that they have, literally, a whole world of flower material at their disposal. Colour awareness and competence in the use of this abundant material cannot be learnt in the same way as one can grasp the basic technique of wiring. But when you have mastered the rules, try to apply them, then be more venturesome and experiment according to your own inclinations. You have the whole world of colour at your finger tips.

CHAPTER THIRTEEN

Sales Technique

Some people actively enjoy selling things, whilst others dislike the mere thought of it. But what, in fact, is selling, other than an exchange of ideas? For example, you are interested in something that you believe someone else might also enjoy. So you tell them about it. It may be the film you saw last night, it might be a new kind of breakfast food you think they would like to try, or it could be that you want your family to meet a new friend of yours. In each case, you are selling your point of view, in a manner of speaking.

How many times have we all said 'I'll try to persuade him to do so and so.' This means that you have an idea or a point of view in which you believe, and you propose trying to make someone else share this view.

This is nothing like so cold-blooded as it sounds. It goes on all the time. Whenever you express a point of view about something, you are unconsciously selling this thing about which *you* have a point of view.

And having a point of view about something usually means that you know something about it. So that in order to sell flowers and flower design with confidence, you first have to learn something about it all.

This can be quite a lengthy process which, over the years, will add up to valuable experience. But it need not take too long to get to know the sort of flowers stocked in your shop, the prices of flowers and accessories and, of course, the prices of designs.

Referring for a moment back to the first paragraph – you would, presumably, only attempt to 'sell' your point of view to someone you knew fairly well. For example, you would hardly be likely to go up to a total stranger in the street and say: 'Do you know, you really should make an effort to see such-and-such a film, or eat so-and-so's breakfast food'. One can imagine what might happen if everyone went around doing this! But selling in a flower shop will, however, inevitably mean that you will be speaking to people who, for the most part, will be total strangers to you.

Selling – and buying – flowers is rather a personal business. Very few people buy flowers in the same way as they buy toothpaste – because the last lot has been used up. They buy flowers for all sorts of personal reasons. For birthdays, anniversaries, to express thanks, sympathy, joy or sorrow – all these very personal feelings come to the surface when someone walks into your flower shop.

It may be that they know exactly what they want and are able to say so clearly. In which case, there is very little sales problem at all. But on the other hand, they might simply know that they need flowers, and then your job is to help them make a good choice relative to what they can afford to pay.

A definition of the good sale is satisfaction to both parties. This means that the person buying should feel happy with what he or she has bought, and also with the price paid. The person selling should feel he has received a fair price for the goods. It could be that your sales talk is so smooth that you persuade your client to spend almost twice as much money as he intended. But as he goes out of the shop he might think: 'my goodness, I can't afford that sort of extravagance more than once in a lifetime!' Although you will have rung a respectable sum into the cash register, you would also have rung a warning bell in your client's mind. He will remember you, not as the florist who sold him good flowers, but as the person who made him spend more money than he could really afford.

You can also have the exact opposite of this situation, too. A client may have a rough idea of what he is wanting, and also approximately of the price. This is the tricky bit – if you suggest a price that is too low, he might be offended. Therefore it is more tactful to ask 'how many flowers.? How large a design? Is it wanted for something very special?' Never, but never, 'how much did you want to pay?' This thoughtless and tactless remark could be the deathknell of the happy and satisfactory sale.

All this might give the impression that selling is a very complicated operation. However, if you analyse it, it really boils down to common civility with a little bit of human sympathy and hospitality thrown in for good measure. When a client enters your shop, of course you will welcome him with a smile. At this stage, you do not know what he has come to buy. It might be flowers for a happy occasion, on the other hand, it could be that he has to place a funeral order. So the first thing you must do is to listen, and listen carefully. If it is going to be a sale that you feel certain you can handle efficiently, go right ahead and do your best. But if you feel uncertain for any

reason, ask the client to be kind enough to wait whilst
you (*a*) ask advice, or (*b*) bring someone more senior to
help.

If you are selling cut flowers, handle each flower as if
you had paid for it yourself. The more carefully you
handle the stock, the more important the flowers will
appear in the eyes of your customer. Learn to wrap
flowers efficiently. Remember that the stems will be full
of water and when you take them from the display vases,
hold them immediately head downwards. Hand the
wrapped parcel to your customer with the flower heads
downwards, otherwise the water will run from the stems
and make the wrapping paper damp and soggy.

Booking an Order. Make sure that you fully understand
the order sheets in use in your shop. Certain very important
details must always be noted. To book and execute an
order you need:

1. The full name and address of the recipient (the
   person who is going to receive the flowers). Remember
   here that ladies in hospital are listed under their *own*
   Christian name, not that of their husband. Thus,
   you should write – 'Mrs Margaret Jones' not 'Mrs
   Richard Jones'.

2. Full details of the order, types of flowers and price,
   itemising all charges, delivery, etc.

3. The day, date and possibly the time of delivery.
   Normally, only weddings and funerals are delivered
   to a specific time, but make quite sure what the
   practice is in your particular shop, before you
   promise a timed delivery.

4. If your client writes a card to go with the order, put it in an envelope and write the full address clearly on the outside and fix it firmly to the order. If the client gives you the message to write, do this as carefully as you know how. If your writing is not all it might be, ask someone else to do this for you. A badly-written card will diminish the appearance of an order.

5. The full name and address of your client and, if possible, telephone number.

Handle the booked order with as much care as you handle the flowers for a cash sale. Never scribble or write hurriedly. Try to print all names and place-names. People very much dislike having their names spelt wrongly.

When you have written out the order, go over it again with the customer to double-check it. There are bound to be moments when you need help from more senior staff. Never hesitate to ask. A customer will have much more patience with someone who says that he or she must go and ask, than with a sales-hand who just looks vague and says the first thing that occurs to him.

There may be a small space on the order form for your own name. If not, just write it somewhere where it can be seen. Clients sometimes refer back to their order, and it is much easier to identify staff by name than for the client to say 'I was waited on by the slim young lady with brown eyes'. There could be three like that in the workroom!

Telephone selling can be described as much the same as shop selling, only more so. When a client is actually in the shop he usually has a moment or so in hand, if you

need to make an enquiry or keep him waiting for anything special – unless, of course, his car is parked on an
expiring parking meter. But on the telephone, every
second counts. Never answer the telephone unless you
have writing materials at hand. It may be long-distance,
even overseas, and your sales technique is not going to
get off to a very good start if you have to say 'please hold
on while I fetch a pencil'.

It is no good answering the telephone unless you know
the prices of the stock. Many shops keep a price list near
the telephone, which saves a lot of running to and fro, and
the inevitable 'just wait while I go and ask'

Always say who you are as soon as you lift the receiver.
You will answer something like this – 'Good morning, this
is Flower Design, Margaret – or George – speaking.' The
client will appreciate this personal touch which will give
him confidence in the efficiency of your shop.

The client then knows your identity as soon as you
answer the bell. But at this stage you have no idea who is
on the other end of the line. If he should ask to speak to a
particular person on the firm, never just say 'hold on, I'll
go and find him or her'. Always ask the caller's name.
Also by saying you will go to find the person, you have
implied that he or she is, in fact, on the premises. It is not
reasonable to expect your employer or one of his senior
staff to drop whatever they may be doing to come to the
telephone to speak to an unknown voice.

Be sure you get the caller's name right and then say
you will go to see if the person wanted is free. Many
florists now do more than fifty per cent of their business by
telephone, so be sure that you never pick up the receiver

unless you know at least a good many of the answers.

Finally, imagine that you are using, not a telephone, but television. Your voice is the only thing you have to convey your personality on the telephone. This instrument, splendid though it is, is apt to flatten voices and make them very impersonal. Female voices, in particular, are apt to lose a lot of their personality unless one makes quite an effort. So put a welcoming smile in your voice by wearing a real smile. The caller won't, of course, be able to *see* your smile, but he will *sense* it through your telephone voice, which must be warm, confident and smiling.

CHAPTER FOURTEEN

How to Train as a Florist

It is not always easy to decide what career to follow, particularly if you happen to be one of those people who usually finish up more or less in the middle of the marking list at examinations. If you get high marks in one or two subjects and, perhaps, very low ones in others, then this will probably give you a clue as to where your capabilities lie.

What school subjects are, in fact, most likely to be helpful to you in Floristry? Obviously, Botany, Biology, English, Art and Modern Languages come high on the list, but in point of fact, all school subjects eventually come in useful. You may wonder what on earth is the point of learning Latin, but a basis in this subject will help you to remember much more easily the horticultural names of the plant material. It is also essential to be able to write clearly and neatly, and many students who have specialised in Art write particularly well. It makes such a difference to the appearance of the flower shop when tickets, labels, delivery lists and greeting cards are written attractively, and a student florist can often be made responsible for this work.

Why Modern Languages? The go-ahead flower designer needs to know something of the work of florists in other countries, and to be able to introduce new ideas into the shop. The ideal thing is to spend some time working abroad during your career, and obviously to do this you must be able to speak a little of the language, otherwise you would find yourself completely isolated. A basic knowledge to O-level is all that is needed, as you would soon learn to speak fluently when working all day and hearing nothing but, say, French or German spoken.

Games and P.T. also add up to something very useful in the initial training of a student flower designer. It may also seem strange to think of such subjects in relation to floristry, but in the flower industry you need to be quite agile and strong. If you are fond of sport generally and enjoy plenty of activity, then this is the life for you. Very little of the florist's day is spent sitting down, in fact, most of them seem to prefer to stand even when they *could* sit down.

If you happen to have a friend or someone in the family who is connected with the world of flowers, then it has no doubt already been suggested to you as a possible career. Whilst you are still at school ask your Careers Master or Mistress for the booklet called *Careers with Flowers* which gives you the up-to-date information on the industry. There is also a list in it of horticultural institutes and schools of floristry where you could have some initial training. If the booklet is not at your school, write yourself to the Secretary of the British Flower Industry Association, 35 Wellington Street, Covent Garden, London, W.C.2.

Having made some general enquiries and studied the *Careers with Flowers* booklet, you will then want to begin making plans. The obvious person to help you is a florist. If you happen to know one in your area, go and see him and ask his help. The British Flower Industry Association could also help and may, possibly, be able to give you the names and addresses of florists who, they know, are willing to accept students.

If, on the other hand, you know of a flower shop that, for some reason or other, makes you feel as if you would like to work there, write a letter to the owner or manager giving particulars of your age, which school you attend, what subjects you have studied and to what level, and ask if you may call to see about working there. Most florists are fairly sympathetic people – the very nature of their business dictates that they shall be – and even if the shop you write to does not have room for a student at the moment, they may be able to suggest the name of a colleague who could accept you.

This is what is known as going in on the ground floor – in other words, you will have no formal training in floristry at this stage, and you will therefore be working and learning at the same time. If there is a day-release course in the vicinity, then your employer would probably want you to take advantage of it.

If, however, it is possible for you to do some formal training when you leave school, this is naturally the better thing to do. You should then reach a recognised standard and you would, naturally, be more useful to the work-room than you would be if you went into it straight from school.

Q. Is it necessary to have some Horticultural training?

A. It is by no means essential, but if you are able to spare the time for this training first, it will eventually add up to something very useful indeed. Floristry is so much easier when you understand how and where the plant material is grown. It certainly helps to make a better flower designer, because your knowledge of flowers and plants will give you a greater insight into the nature and suitability of the materials you will be using. This knowledge will help you give added personality and interest to your designs and lift them from the ordinary to the unique.

Q. Would I have to go away from home for training?

A. Many of the colleges of Horticulture have residential courses, and for people who have been to a day school, this can be a very interesting experience. You would be training with other people of your own age, with similar interests. You would probably be living during term-time in another part of the country. Moreover, most of these colleges also include a certain amount of training on packing and marketing as well as production. This makes an excellent background for floristry. The training usually lasts a minimum of one year.

Q. Would there be any difference in my wages if I have had initial training of some sort before going into a flower shop?

A. This would depend on the standard you reach. Initial training should mean that you learn much more quickly when you go into a flower shop, and your rise in status and wages should therefore be quicker than if you 'earn as you learn'.

Q. Are there any examinations that I can take?

A. In Horticulture, there are the examinations of the Royal

This should give you some ideas on how to train for and enter the Flower industry. Unlike some careers, it does not call for a wide range of expensive tools. Similar to other careers, the better qualified you are, the better and more interesting job you can get. It is one of those jobs where individuality and imagination can become a part of your qualifications. You need never feel as if you are a tiny cog in a huge commercial machine, because the success of so many transactions will, in fact, depend on you and you alone. If you make a success of selling a bunch of flowers, your client will be happy and will return for more. If you make a pleasing design, this, too, will please the client. And, although you will at first be working under direction, most things that you do will probably be improved by the application of a little of your own personality.

Incidentally, it is one of the few industries that is unlikely to be greatly affected by automation. True, on the production side, things are becoming more streamlined, but in the flower shops, it is very unlikely that machines could ever take the place of the creative artist or the sympathetic sales staff.

Acknowledgements

I would like to thank the following for kind permission to use their photographs:

The Flowers and Plants Council for plates 3, 4, 8, 9, and 13.

The Associated Bulb Growers of Holland for plates 1, 5, 7, 11 and 15.

The Times for plate 2.

Index

units, 70
Flowering plants, 84
Flowers, 15, 20, 26
Foam base, 15, 53
Focal point, 49, 51
Foliage, 20, 26, 32, 58
Foliage plants, 84
France, 29
Frames, 14, 19
Freesia, 14, 30, 40, 41, 56, 94
Funeral designs, 19
    director, 76
    sheaves, 15, 47
    spray, 82
    tributes, 14, 16, 26, 43

Gardenia, 42, 43
Garnette rose, 71
Gauge, 13, 14, 33, 36
Gates of Heaven, 24
Gifts, 26
Gladioli, 20, 26, 29, 54, 55
Green, 99
Guttapercha, 15, 46

Hair grips, 75
Hamamelis mollis, 94
Hand towel, 16
Harmony, 52
Harp, 24
Head-dresses, 67, 73
Heather, 91
Hedera carnariensis, 86
Holland, 27
Holly, 95
Hyacinth, 14, 33, 41, 42, 71, 92
Hydrangea, 31, 32, 43, 92, 94

Informal sheaf, 79
Interior wiring, 36
    hook method, 42
Iris, 21, 29, 33, 38, 49, 56
   reticulata, 92

Kalanchoe, 91
Knives, 16

Larkspur, 94
Lateral, 50, 51
Latin, 108
Light, 29
Lilac, 30, 31
Lily-of-the-valley (convallaria), 14,
   39
Line, 56
Lupin, 94

Mechanics, 53
Mesh, 24
Method, 17, 20
Memorial Cross, 21
Mimosa, 32
Modern languages, 108
Monochromatic colour, 97
Moss, 20
Mossing, 19
Mounting, 33, 43

Narcissus, 30, 43, 92
Net ribbon, 68
Node, 34, 38
Nursery, 26

Open heart, 23
Orange, 99
Orchid, 33
Outline, 48, 55
Overall (trouser suit), 10
Oxford Dictionary, 47

Packing, 61
Paper white, 43
Pelargonium, 92
Peperomia, 88
Pillow, 22
Pinking shears, 17

115